WRESTLING WITH
FATHERHOOD

WRESTLING WITH
FATHERHOOD

MY CHAMPIONSHIP JOURNEY TO MY GREATEST TITLE: DAD

TITUS O'NEIL

WITH PAUL GUZZO

Published by ECW Press
665 Gerrard Street East
Toronto, Ontario, Canada M4M 1Y2
416-694-3348 / info@ecwpress.com

Editor for the Press: Michael Holmes
Copy-editor: Laura Pastore
All photos couresty of Thaddeus Bullard
Cover by WWE

To the best of his abilities, the author has related experiences, places, people, and organizations from his memories of them. In order to protect the privacy of others, he has, in some instances, changed the names of certain people and details of events and places.

LIBRARY AND ARCHIVES CANADA CATALOGUING
IN PUBLICATION

Title: Wrestling with fatherhood : my championship journey to my greatest title: Dad / Titus O'Neil; with Paul Guzzo.

Names: O'Neil, Titus, author. | Guzzo, Paul, author.

Identifiers: Canadiana (print) 20240398467 | Canadiana (ebook) 20240398475

ISBN 978-1-77041-761-8 (softcover)
ISBN 978-1-77852-322-9 (ePub)
ISBN 978-1-77852-323-6 (PDF)

Subjects: LCSH: O'Neil, Titus. | LCSH: O'Neil, Titus—Family. | LCSH: Father and child. | LCSH: Wrestlers—United States—Biography. | LCGFT: Autobiographies.

Classification: LCC HQ756 .O54 2024 | DDC 306.874/2—dc23

PRINTED AND BOUND IN CANADA

PRINTING: FRIESENS   5   4   3   2   1

To my children, Titus, T.J., and Leah Bullard, three amazing, talented, loving, and compassionate human beings whom I continue to be in awe of how great they are soaring in all aspects of life beyond my wildest dreams.

CONTENTS

FOREWORD

I n my line of work, I have had the opportunity to meet and collaborate with some of the finest human beings across the globe, including kings, world leaders, and celebrities. But what I value most in a person is not their accomplishments, wealth, or fame. What I value most is who they are when the cameras are not on, when no one is watching, and when their hearts are not fully on display for others to see.

I have been around Thaddeus Bullard in the most public settings: galas, sporting events, dinners, et cetera. I've also witnessed Thaddeus in the quietest moments when he is around his close friends and family or when it's just the two of us. Thaddeus is the same person no matter where he is or who he interacts with. His giving spirit and his gratitude for the life that he lives is authentically Thad.

Thaddeus sits at the top of the list of people I value most because of who he is even when no one else is around. But more importantly, because of the three extraordinary children he has raised. These young adults lead their lives with kindness, generosity, and integrity—all qualities upon which Thaddeus's legacy is built.

A Bible verse in Matthew 7 states, "You will know them by their fruits." If you see a tree and want to know its type, you don't have to collect a soil sample, test its bark, or identify its leaves. All you have to do is look at its fruit. The true test of a father—the type of person that he is—is the fruit that he bears.

That love does not just manifest itself through his children. Thaddeus's love can be found in the community, in the father figure he has become to children who do not have one. In a world where parents struggle to take ownership and responsibility for their children, Thaddeus enthusiastically steps into that role and inspires us all to be greater fathers.

His children are the product of his love. Our community's children are the product of his love. And we are all benefactors of his fruit.

Will Packer

Two-time Emmy-nominated producer and one of
Hollywood's most influential record-breaking filmmakers

CHAPTER 1

FATHER'S DAY

F ather's Day: one of the most celebrated holidays everywhere. It's a day when fathers are pampered, treated like royalty, showered with love and gifts and reminded of how much they mean to their family and matter to the world.

It's the ultimate stamp of approval: *Yeah, Dad, you're awesome.* Oh, wait, sorry, that's Mother's Day.

Tradition says you give mothers flowers and jewelry, go out for a fancy dinner, or cook a grand meal. Question, fellas: have you ever tried to book a dinner reservation for Mother's Day on Mother's Day? Unless you made a reservation weeks or even months in advance, good luck finding a table anywhere. The nearest available reservation is probably somewhere in Antarctica, which for a Florida boy like me—well, cold weather is not my jam.

On the flip side, have you ever tried to book a dinner reservation at a good restaurant on Father's Day? Probably not—probably not the day of or during the weeks prior. A good Father's Day meal is not a national tradition.

You can tell how much thought we put into Father's Day by the gifts: socks and ties. Sometimes we get a new grill, but we all know that present equally benefits the family. Ask yourself: what would happen if Mom was gifted cookware too? There is a pretty good chance the family would have to seek shelter elsewhere. Remember the old saying "Happy wife, happy life"? There is no such saying for dads.

I'm sure I'm not alone in thinking that Father's Day is a secondary holiday to Mother's Day, on par in national importance with Arbor Day.

While Mother's Day is like a name-brand cookie with national commercials, jingles, and colorful characters, Father's Day is like the store-brand cookie wrapped in uninspiring packaging. Sure, they both taste delicious, but if you place the two side by side, there is not a single kid who would want the generic cookie.

Father's Day even gets second billing on the calendar.

Mother's Day is on the second Sunday of May, when school is in session and kids can create cards and homemade gifts in art class. Father's Day, on the other hand, is held the third Sunday of June, when most schools are out for the summer.

So let me revise my earlier statement.

Father's Day is not on par with Arbor Day. Arbor Day is celebrated the last Friday of April, when school is in session and the tree holiday can be observed through both art and science projects. Father's Day falls below Arbor Day.

Obviously, I'm joking and exaggerating, but not totally.

Regardless of its second-class status, my three children do treat Father's Day as a major event, but I know countless dads who say the holiday is like a tree falling in the woods: Sometimes it's celebrated. Sometimes it's ignored.

I have received numerous accolades: Celebrity Dad of the Year, twice nominated for ESPN's Muhammad Ali Sports Humanitarian Award, South Tampa Chamber of Commerce's 2020 Citizen of the Year, grand marshal of the Indy 500, grand marshal of the Krewe of the Knights of Sant'Yago Illuminated Knight Parade in Tampa, WWE Tag Team champion, the first ever to win the WWE 24/7 Championship, and I'm a member of the WWE Hall of Fame as a Warrior Award recipient. I'm blessed.

But being a father is my greatest honor and the greatest title I will ever hold. I have said that since the day my first son was born. Being a father means everything to me.

Before we get too deep into this, let's be clear: I'm not an expert on fatherhood or parenthood. These are solely my opinions based on my experiences as a child, young man, and father and from discussions I have had with fathers of various backgrounds from around the world, who offered their unique perspectives.

I'm writing this book at this point in my life because, lately and for multiple reasons, I have been thinking about fatherhood more than ever.

My oldest son, TJ Bullard, is at college, living his dream, playing Division I football for the University of Central Florida on an athletic scholarship.

By the time you read this, my younger son, Titus Bullard, will either be in college or preparing to leave for college, also playing football on an athletic scholarship.

And in 2023, I officially adopted Leah Bullard, who has been my unofficial daughter since she was seven years old and who, by the time you read this, will also either be at or preparing to leave for college, playing basketball on an athletic scholarship.

I emphasize their athletic scholarships because of the hard work my kids have put in, but also because their private high school education has cost me a lot of money. My kids have given their mother and me the greatest return on investment when it comes to their education: they are earning their way through college. Well, except for food and car insurance and gas . . .

Watching and preparing for my children to leave the nest has me thinking quite a bit about parenting, the sacrifices I have made as a father and my successes and failures. Every parent faces the same question: how do I raise my children with the greatest of love, the strongest of discipline, and the wherewithal to understand their vision of where they want to go in life while also properly investing and guiding them through the process? I'm proud I have put my children in the best position possible to follow their dreams.

And it's not just my kids who have me thinking about fatherhood.

In 2021, the Hillsborough County School District in Florida honored me by renaming the Sligh Middle Magnet School as Thaddeus M. Bullard Academy at Sligh Middle Magnet School. This wasn't done in response to a large check that I wrote. Rather it's to recognize my years of supporting that school, which caters to an underprivileged community. Since 2016, I championed the school financially and as a mentor, and I remain hands-on now that the building bears my name. Part of my work there includes serving as a male role model to children who don't have one at home. I seek to serve as a father figure to whomever needs me and to help fathers looking to become better versions of themselves. That work has me analyzing my advice and actions, questioning if I'm saying and doing the right things.

I'm writing this book because I believe that we, as a society, need to embrace what fatherhood is truly about. Being a great father doesn't depend on whether a man is married, rich, a celebrity, or has millions of social media followers. I have met millionaires whom I would classify as horrible fathers. A great father can be married, divorced, a CEO, working whatever odd jobs that he can find to provide for his children, or someone who stays at home to take care of the kids.

Much like anything in life at which people are great, it must start with a want, a desire that burns inside of them to achieve the greatest level of what it is they want to become. Great athletes operate differently than good athletes. Great teachers operate differently than good teachers. Great businesspeople operate differently than good businesspeople. To be a great father, you must have a great desire and want to be a hero and an inspiration to your child, first and foremost.

We have a slogan in WWE: we put smiles on faces. Being a great father is much like being a WWE Superstar. A great father wants to put a smile on his child's face.

I'm not advocating for fatherhood to be placed on a pedestal above motherhood. But I am advocating for them to be placed on pedestals side by side.

And I'm not saying fathers don't like socks and ties, but I know we would all appreciate a good meal too.

———

Toward the end of my junior year of high school, my mother asked me two questions that were a turning point for me: Would

I like to know the name of the man whose DNA courses through my veins? Would I like help finding him?

I think many would readily say yes. I think many would want to meet the man who helped to create them, get to know him, and form a parent-child bond. But I'm not like most people.

My origin story is different than most.

Just moments before my mother, Daria Bullard, asked those questions, she told me the circumstances of my birth for the first time ever: At 11 years old, she had been raped by an adult male whom she knew and trusted. I was the product of that violent act.

There was a lot to digest that day, but it wasn't enough to cloud my judgment when my mother offered to help unite me with the man who attacked her and stole her innocence and childhood.

I said no.

And I have never regretted that decision.

Sure, I have wondered about him from time to time. I wonder if I look like him. I wonder if I inherited my athleticism from him. I wonder if he knows about me and what I have accomplished. I wonder if he is still alive. But I have never wanted to meet him.

He is not my dad. Don't grace him with such a title. Don't even call him a sperm donor. That man is a predator. That man is a monster. He is not my father.

Charles Blalock is my dad. We don't share an ounce of DNA, but Charles Blalock is the man whom I celebrate every Father's Day.

It's strange that Father's Day means so much to me now. It used to mean so little to me because I had never known my father, and the idea of a father, as a regular part of home life, was alien to me.

My three brothers knew their father, but he left us when we were young. My mother's father wasn't around either; he left her family when she was a kid. So Father's Day meant nothing to me—until I finally had a father.

I was filled with anger as a little kid; I got into fights and talked back to teachers. I believe it was because I didn't have a male role model to set me straight.

From ninth grade through senior year, I lived at Live Oak's Florida Sheriffs Boys Ranch, which provides a long-term nurturing residential environment for at-risk children. By teaching work ethic, self-respect, discipline, and spirituality while the young men and women also attend a local school, it has helped turn around the lives of countless children. I was set to be an outlier. The ranch's tactics worked for others but were not working for me. I struggled to overcome my anger issues.

Then I met Charles Blalock. He was superintendent of Suwannee County (where Live Oak is located), a well-respected civil rights icon, a physical giant of a man, and his son played football at Suwannee High School, where I had a reputation as a troublemaker. But during my freshman year, my teachers saw promise in me, so they asked Mr. Blalock, who mentored young men, to have a talk with me.

He sort of "spoke" with me. It was more like he threatened me, lovingly.

My gym teacher introduced us and then left us alone. Mr. Blalock—standing at six-foot-three and 250 pounds— matter-of-factly told me he could whup me easily, no matter how tough I thought I was, and he would do so if I continued to act out. He wasn't trying to bully me. He was trying to make a point. I had too much anger, and I thought I could get away with it because of my size. But sooner or later I would meet someone bigger and stronger, and then what? He did not want me to learn the hard way and live with the consequences for the rest of my life. He made me a deal: If I continued to cause trouble, he would come back and prove how easy it would be for him to take me on. But if I changed my attitude, he would support me in every way. I promised I would do the right thing.

I lived up to my promise. Mr. Blalock did too.

Despite having three biological children, he brought me into his family. When they went out for dinner, I went too. When they went to the movies, so did I. And when they went out to celebrate Father's Day that year, I celebrated with them.

We didn't do anything huge. We drove to Tallahassee where one of his daughters lived, went out to dinner, and then returned home. But it felt monumental to me. It was the first Father's Day I had ever been a part of.

When Mr. Blalock's son graduated high school at the end of my freshman year, I moved into his room on weekends. My relationship with Mr. Blalock then blossomed to the point that one night, after we returned from a trip to watch a college football game together, I asked if I could call him "Dad." He replied yes, but on one condition: I had to let him call me "Son."

The following June, I walked to the grocery store one day after school to purchase my first Father's Day card. I would like to say that I spent an hour perusing the section, carefully looking for the perfect card. But I just grabbed whatever I saw first and have since forgotten what it said. But I still remember the note that I wrote to him: "Thank you for teaching me how to be a man and accepting me into your family. Happy Father's Day, Dad. Your son, Thaddeus."

———

In the WWE ring, I have been shown up by a bunny and an evil Russian in front of my sons and my hero, the Reverend Jesse Jackson.

Well, technically, *I* wasn't.

I'm Thaddeus Bullard. Titus O'Neil, the WWE Superstar whom I portray on TV, was the one who was shown up.

I always preach that there is a clear divide between myself and my television character. When the cameras are on, I'm Titus O'Neil, the WWE Superstar. Once the cameras are off, I'm Thaddeus Bullard, who embodies the three Fs: fatherhood, foodie and filanthropist . . . uh, okay, philanthropist—two Fs and one Ph.

But there are also times when WWE blurs those lines by incorporating part of my life into Titus O'Neil's scripted storylines. The storylines with the bunny and the evil Russian, for example. But, more importantly, those two storylines bolstered my belief that being a father is a far more important title than any I could win with WWE.

In 2014, I received the Rainbow PUSH Coalition's Humanitarian & Community Service Award.

The Rainbow PUSH Coalition describes itself as an international and civil rights organization founded by Rev. Jackson. It seeks to empower people through the effective use of grassroots advocacy, issue orientation, and by connecting those between the greater community and the disenfranchised. They do so through inner-city youth programs that emphasize education and job placement, by pushing for major corporations to embrace affirmative action, and by advocating for peaceful civil rights protests such as prayer vigils and boycotts.

I was nominated for my work in programs such as the Be a STAR (Show Tolerance and Respect) anti-bullying campaign, the Special Olympics, the Susan G. Komen Breast Cancer Foundation, and my own charities in my hometown of Tampa through the Bullard Family Foundation.

I don't do community work for the recognition. I do it because I feel it's the right thing to do. I do it because, as a minority, I want to be a positive role model who shows other minorities that they too can achieve anything. I do what I do because that is my purpose on Earth: to help change as many lives as possible. I do it because my life was changed through the support of other people.

Sometimes, however, it's nice to be recognized. The publicity might inspire others to support my work or give back to their own community.

The award was also nice because my sons were little kids at the time, and I hope it served as another example that being a serviceman and a servant to others far outweighs the legacy that I can leave as an athlete and entertainer. I can be a WWE Superstar for only a certain period of time, whereas I can be a contributing body to society for my entire life.

The honor was made even bigger because I was nominated by Rev. Jackson himself.

He is obviously a civil rights icon. But he has also always fought for the equality of all people, not just people of color. I strive to do the same. He is a man who has set goals. Some he has reached. Some he has not. But he continues to push for equality among all people.

In short, humbly speaking, the award was a big deal to me.

WWE thought so too, so they incorporated it into a storyline. That is not something unique to me.

WWE Superstars are among the most selfless entertainers in the world. Many of us seek to give back, and WWE promotes that work during shows, like how John Cena has granted more wishes for the Make-A-Wish Foundation than anyone else.

I received the PUSH award at a Chicago ceremony in July 2014. Two months later, *Monday Night Raw* was in Chicago and Rev. Jackson came to the show to support me. My sons were there too. It was a big night.

Rev. Jackson was then incorporated into the storyline.

The announcers boasted about my Rainbow PUSH Coalition Humanitarian & Community Service Award. Rev. Jackson and I filmed a backstage segment together during which he spoke of my community service and called me "a big pussycat." Rev. Jackson was right, but he is also the only non-family member who could get away with calling me that on global television.

Later that night, I had a tag team match. At that time, I was one half of Slater Gator. I was the Gator because I formerly played football and was once the student body vice president for the University of Florida, *the* premier college in the Sunshine State. And Slater was Heath Slater, one of the all-time funniest dudes inside the ring.

The Rev. Jackson and my sons were at ringside to cheer me on, though sitting separately.

There is one thing for certain about WWE. While they don't mind incorporating real life into storylines, they will not let real life change the script. Slater Gator wasn't there to get over. We were there to get others over.

Slater Gator won the match, beating Los Matadores when Heath Slater scored a pinfall.

But in WWE, the pinfall doesn't always mean the match is over, and those post-match shenanigans are often the most entertaining part of the segment.

This is where things got a bit wild. We had a mascot dressed as an alligator. They had a mascot dressed as a bull. After the match, our gator tried to eat their bull. Only in WWE!

Then Adam Rose stormed into the ring. Rose was the "party guy," always seen hanging out with a bizarre cast of characters known as Rosebuds, one of whom was a grown man dressed in a bunny costume.

Well, Rose tossed me from the ring and the bunny took care of Heath Slater. Then the bunny, and not me, celebrated at ringside with Rev. Jackson. I was later asked if I was upset by that ending and that I did not get a chance to shine with my hero while my sons watched on.

Emphatically, no. It's show business.

The crowd had a good time and enjoyed the moment. That is what matters most while I'm on camera for WWE. Besides, I also had one of my all-time favorite parenting memories that week and that far outweighs anything else that happened while in Chicago.

My sons flew up a few days prior to the show to spend time with me. One night, we stepped outside so they could play in the snow for the first time. We had a snowball fight. I let them win, which is rare. I'm so competitive, I would not even let them win in checkers. But I had a televised match coming up and figured missing it due to a slip and fall during a snowball fight would not have been acceptable. So I served more as a stationary target.

My sons have come with me to countless WWE events, and we have traveled to see sporting events and concerts around the world. Yet, when asked, they say their favorite on-the-road moment is experiencing their first snowfall and snowball fight.

The following year, I was honored once again, this time as the Celebrity Dad of the Year, presented by the Everything for Dads Foundation, which assists men in becoming better fathers through online and in-person programs.

With the help of endorsements from Vince and Stephanie McMahon, Triple H, and my best friend and brother, David Bautista, I beat out Ashton Kutcher, Vin Diesel, and David Beckham, three talented, *almost* as successful men whom I'm much better looking than . . .

The foundation touted a public service advertisement that I filmed for the National Responsible Fatherhood Clearinghouse and the Ad Council that featured me playing cards with my two sons and reminding fathers to take the time to be a dad.

As a winner, they had me write my fatherhood mission statement, which was then shared with the world:

> *Fatherhood is the greatest responsibility and honor a man can have placed upon him. I never met my biological father, nor did I grow up with a male figure in my home. I didn't grow up with money, a nice home, or fancy clothes. In fact, I spent the majority of my childhood living in the projects or with family members. However, thanks to my mom, I had no*

shortage of love. Because of that, I feel very strongly that love, faith, strength, and courage are the most important elements of growing and learning at any stage of life. Now, as a father, I strive to demonstrate these in my home because the greatest lesson my kids have taught me is how to love people unconditionally.

Being a father has allowed me to keep things in perspective, for which I'm extremely grateful. When a young fan asks for an autograph or picture or when I visit hospitals and schools, I always think, "What if these were my kids? What if my children were sick or didn't have the resources to obtain a great education, live in a safe neighborhood, or live a comfortable life?" I'm very grateful when people go the extra mile for my kids, and I make it a point to always return that favor. Life as a WWE Superstar is hectic and stressful at times, but the ability to positively change lives on a daily basis motivates me to work hard. My kids could not care less if I win or lose a match or if I have a bad day at work. I have come to find not just my kids but WWE fans love and respect me regardless because beyond the lights, cameras, and the action in the ring, they continue to see a real, genuine person. My philosophy with my kids is simple . . . I expect them to do their best and be the best people they can be, and they expect the same of me.

To me, being a father is simple. I live for my kids, not through my kids. I'm not trying to force them into doing the things I did as a child in sports or extra-curricular activities because they are who God made *them to be. As their father, my job is to provide my children with the best positive guidance, motivation, discipline, and resources possible to help them reach their greatness. I do this with plenty of love and try to be a living example instead of a telling example. I have learned kids respond more to what they see you do, as opposed to what you tell them to do. I'm their first role model, and I take that very seriously. They might not take the same path I did, but as long as they respect people, work hard, are positive about life, and give their absolute best effort, I always will be proud of them.*

To me, the most important part of being a father is being present. Kids really remember the moments and time you spend with them more than the things you buy them. The smallest moments make the biggest impact on a child's life. I often am asked what I like most about being a father, and my answer is always that I love everything about being a father: the challenges, the responsibility, the discipline, the laughter, the school functions . . . you name it, I love it. Father's Day is really a special day, but for me, every day is Father's Day because I get another day to enjoy all of the wonderful characteristics my two sons display. I also get to be part of a very great fraternity . . . FATHERHOOD! I'm honored, humbled, and proud to be a father.

WWE again boasted my accolade and incorporated it into a storyline.

I have never missed one Father's Day with my children. WWE typically has a live event that weekend, but I have always flown my kids out to spend time with them.

The 2016 *Money in the Bank* show was held on Father's Day, and I took Rusev on in a match that I knew, from the moment it was booked, I would be slated to lose. Rusev was the new monster title contender being built up by WWE. And the best way to build someone up as a monster is by putting them in the ring with another big man whom they vanquish.

Again, it's show business.

It was a pretty competitive match. I landed some good punches and elbows, tossed Rusev into the barricade, and hit a pump handle powerslam. But he ultimately forced me to submit to his accolade, a modern-day camel clutch.

Again, here is where things got crazy.

My sons were at ringside, and Rusev got right in their faces and screamed, "Happy Father's Day!" Again I was asked if that bothered me. I was father of the year, it was Father's Day, and I said "I quit" in front of my kids, who were then taunted by the victor. Also, Rev. Jackson was in the crowd again.

Once again, I emphatically said no. It was a show and what better way to build Rusev than to have him taunt my sons.

My oldest, TJ, might have gotten a bit too into it. He slapped Rusev. That wasn't part of the script. Luckily, the character Rusev and the man who portrayed him are nothing alike.

My sons had a blast being a part of an angle, which is why, despite losing the match, it's my second all-time favorite Father's Day memory, and my sons echo that sentiment.

As for my first . . .

I was in the bathroom when I learned I would be a father. It wasn't exactly a scene ripped from a family movie, but real life rarely is.

Unbeknownst to me at the time, my then-wife, Alle, had been feeling nauseous that day. We had not been trying to have a baby, but we had not exactly *not* been trying either. When she did not have a fever or any other symptoms, she decided to buy a pregnancy test.

I was getting ready to go out for the evening, and I rushed into the bathroom without knocking. I excused myself when I saw Alle on the toilet, but then quickly noticed she was sitting on the closed seat, fully clothed. She was also holding a pregnancy test, crying tears of joy.

"We are pregnant," she happily exclaimed.

I wept too.

I was so excited.

I was excited to become their hero.

I was excited to teach them to become an adult.

I was excited to become their Mr. Blalock.

I called my mother first with the news.

Next was Mr. Blalock. His response: "I'm so proud of you, Son. You are going to be a great father."

I was living in Fort Myers, Florida, but playing in the Arena Football League for the Las Vegas Gladiators at the time, so I could not be home as often as I wanted during the pregnancy. But my family, friends, and colleagues rallied around my wife as a supportive base for our first child.

Still, despite the practice and travel schedule, I was there for major sonogram milestones, most importantly the first heartbeat and learning the baby was a boy. We instantly decided on Thaddeus Michael Bullard Jr. as his name, though everyone now calls him TJ, as in Thaddeus Junior.

On June 16, 2004, at 7 a.m., at 38 weeks pregnant, Alle was scheduled to be induced. We packed her bags, made phone calls, and prepared our apartment so it would be ready for our return with a new and tiny member of the family.

After 10 hours in a Cape Coral Hospital delivery room, TJ still refused to come out into the world, which is ironic because he became a young man who prefers to be out in the world rather than home. The doctor said we had come to a stopping point, where Mom and baby were exhausted, and the alternative of the C-section was the best option. We agreed, and they began to prepare my wife. Prep meant needles. And needles meant my knees began to buckle. Yes, I'm not afraid to put my health and wellness on the line inside a WWE ring, but I'm terrified of needles.

The surgery went perfectly, TJ was pulled from his mother, and his whines brought immediate tears to my eyes. I was a father.

The doctor then handed me the umbilical cord and scissors, which brought more tears to my eyes, for a different and grosser reason. But I did my fatherly duty and cut the cord. It was difficult to stomach but, in retrospect, my first job as a father was likely the easiest.

I then internally exclaimed, "Thank you, Jesus! We have a son."

He was delivered at 7:05 p.m. on June 16, 2004, and was seven pounds, 16 ounces, and 19 inches long. At that moment, I never could have imagined how much bigger he would get.

Calls were made throughout Florida and as far away as Las Vegas to announce TJ's safe delivery and passage into the world. TJ's maternal uncle, Earnest Graham, who was playing football for the Tampa Bay Bucs, made a drive down to Cape Coral that night to see his second-born nephew, to welcome him into the world, and to congratulate us. The next day, the grandmothers arrived with kisses and giggles. Even his great grandmother made the trip to meet TJ.

TJ and his mother were supposed to remain at the hospital for 48 hours, but that was extended to 96 due to slight complications. And that meant my first-born son was to come home on June 20, 2004, which was Father's Day.

I did not rest much the night before TJ came home. I instead made a lot of calls, asking questions about being a first-time dad. I talked to my dad, Charles Blalock, my mom, my coach, and some friends. It was definitely overwhelming and exciting to take on and take in. I knew one thing: I was going to be the best father to my son, my namesake. God had given me a gift who totally relied upon and depended on me as a man and a role model. I had to deliver.

It did not take long for me to falter.

The next day at the hospital, I made it to the fifth floor before realizing I had forgotten the car seat. I had only realized my mistake because I saw another father walking with his and trying to figure it out. That was my only job that morning. Way to go, Dad! So I returned to my car, retrieved the car seat, and proceeded back to the hospital room as if I was a father who had it all together.

Once in the room, I could not believe my eyes. My son's hospital carriage name tag said "Thaddeus Michael Bullard II" and included an imprint of his tiny feet. "This is really happening," I thought. "I have a son. I'm a father. Man, this is the best day of my life!"

As I stood in the doorway, I looked over at his mother and, with tears in my eyes, walked over to her bed, gave her a hug, and gently kissed her forehead. She gave me an update on how our newborn baby slept through the night and how he nursed every two hours. She was tired, and the surgery had taken a toll on her body.

I was so anxious to hold my son again but had to wait because he had just returned from his circumcision and the nurse was now giving instructions on how to clean him, put a diaper on him, care for his navel, and on and on. I wanted to scream, "Hurry it up!" I just wanted to hold my son. But there were so many instructions for caring for him and his mother, so many dos and don'ts, and so many more doctor appointments for me to remember for both Mom and baby.

Finally, it was time for us to leave, bring my son home, and kick off our lives together.

But TJ started crying. I walked over to see if I could figure out why he was fussing, but I was at a loss. The nurse told me to gently check if he was wet or if he had a poopy diaper, and guess what? He was wet *and* he had a poopy diaper.

I had changed plenty of diapers before. Growing up in South Florida, kids typically babysat themselves in groups. We would be left at one home or apartment, and the older ones would be charged with caring for the babies.

But this felt different. For some reason, I was nervous.

I wanted to look TJ in the eyes and say, "Now hold on, Junior, you cannot do your daddy like that already. Let me at least get you home and watch your mom change you a couple of times."

Thankfully, the nurse could see the "new dad" look on my face and kindly changed him for me. His mom just shook her head, laughed, and reminded me I had to do it sooner or later. Never one to back down, not even from a joke, I teased that I wasn't changing any diapers, well, not the poopy ones anyway. I would feed, burp, and bathe, but a dirty diaper wasn't on my list.

Finally, we were in the car and ready to go home.

Both Mom and TJ were in the backseat, and I began looking at them both from the rearview mirror of my car.

Alle looked back at me and said, "Happy Father's Day."

And that, of course, is my favorite Father's Day memory.

Oh yeah, TJ pooped again later that day. And again and again and again and again. During one of those agains, I caved and changed him. That was the first of many, many, many more.

CHAPTER 2

FATHERLY FEAR

I t really takes a village to weather a storm, but it takes faith to make it through. No one could have prepared us for our new bundle of joy, nor the storm after. The stress of parenthood, especially early parenthood, is real. How you handle that stress is important for your mental and physical health.

Let's rewind to when Alle was pregnant with TJ.

While I was on and off the road playing for the Las Vegas Gladiators, Alle was leading the search for what we thought would be our forever home in Fort Myers. We had several options to choose from and just a couple of weeks to decide before TJ was due.

The pressure of home buying is one thing. Add a pregnancy and the unforeseen adventures that come with welcoming a new human being into the world, and the pressure can sometimes feel overwhelming.

Midway through the pregnancy, we welcomed our first complication. Today, TJ stars on the gridiron. But while he was living inside his mom's belly, he seemed destined for a career as a soccer player, or maybe a WWE Superstar who uses Shawn Michaels's finishing maneuver—a kick to the face known as Sweet Chin Music. At around the 22nd week of her pregnancy, TJ began kicking up a storm. He delivered so many kicks that his mother began experiencing contractions that caused premature labor.

I had just finished playing an arena football game in Colorado when I realized I had several missed calls from Alle, explaining that she was heading to the hospital because her contractions were three or four minutes apart.

She was rushed to Cape Coral Hospital, but they were unable to stop the contractions and were not equipped to handle premature births. So she was then rushed by ambulance to HealthPark Medical Center to prepare for a delivery.

At HealthPark, doses of medicine were given to prepare and strengthen TJ's lungs in the event that they could not stop the birth. Other doses of medicine were given to maintain his stay in the womb for as long as possible, hopefully for a long time. But there was no guarantee he would stay put or be healthy if delivered early.

In the meantime, I caught a red-eye flight from Colorado to be by their side in Florida. On the plane, all I could do was pray. I prayed for her and prayed for him. As much as I had gone through in life, I wasn't prepared for this. Even though I only knew TJ through ultrasound images and the sound of his heartbeat, I already felt a bond with him. I stayed up at night picturing our relationship. I imagined us tossing the football back and forth not long after he learned to stand on his own. I envisioned us going to the movies and sporting events together. I could hear myself dispelling upon him the same advice that my dad, Mr. Blalock, had dispelled upon me. I could not imagine losing TJ if there was a complication due to his early birth—I could not fathom a life without him. Even though his physical body had not entered the Earth, we had a spiritual connection.

But I could not do anything; I was helpless. As a father during pregnancy, you want to be Superman to your child and the mother. But there is almost nothing you can do for either. You are more of a Clark Kent. I was nervous, yet I wasn't going to let fear overcome me. I had to be brave for Alle.

I arrived at the hospital just in time. The doctors were doing all they could medically to convince TJ to stay put. If that failed, they would begin prepping for TJ's delivery.

As I sat by her side, Alle was holding an ultrasound picture of TJ with tears in her eyes. She was praying for him to be okay. I prayed too, but for both the baby and her to be okay. Then, out of nowhere, she pointed at the ultrasound picture and said, "Look, look, TJ is in God's hand!" I first wondered if she was losing her mind. But I looked closer at the image and realized she was correct. In the gray areas of the ultrasound picture, you could see a silhouette of a hand holding our son. If there was ever a moment when we needed reassurance, it was surely then, and God responded and answered our prayers.

Of course, all my bravery dissipated when the medical staff walked in with those needles. I can play football or perform for WWE in front of 100,000 fans without a care in the world. I never buckle under the pressure of a crowd. But needles? Yeah, they buckle my knees. And I had to close my eyes when they jabbed those needles into Alle's belly. I squeezed her hand tight because I needed reassurance, not because I was reassuring her.

Everything turned out okay.

I'm so thankful for the prayers and modern medicine that maintained TJ's home in the womb for 16 more weeks.

Alle then returned home, on bed rest, to a host of family and friends. Former teammates and colleagues assured me that I could return to Las Vegas to finish the football season. And Alle and God reassured me that everything would be okay.

God was true to his word.

Alle? She wasn't done scaring me.

It was the end of spring, and we were headed toward summertime in Florida, when it's either extremely hot or, due to regular downpours, wet. I had returned to my non–football season job as a high school counselor for a nonprofit community Christian school, and I had also taken over searching neighborhoods to find our new home. As Alle approached the last trimester of her pregnancy, the appointments became weekly because she was high risk for premature delivery. Her mother blamed it on me and my genetics. Ha. We still lovingly argue about genetics, both staking claim to my sons' athleticism. But I stand by my claim that my genes are more dominant. My sons are tall. Her family is short.

Anyway, fast-forward to Alle's 36th week of pregnancy. She was on strict bed rest due to swelling. All antennas were up, and so were the phone calls from family who wanted to keep a close watch so that they could be with us at a moment's notice.

I appreciated the calls but was also slightly bothered by them. Everybody was asking about her, but no one seemed concerned about my well-being. Yes, Alle's stress was a billion times greater than mine, and she had stress on both her body and mind. But I was stressed nonetheless and needed someone I could unburden my concerns to. I wasn't going to bring it up on my own. I needed someone to pump my mental well to get the words flowing. When no one did, the stress sat and hardened in my gut.

Life kept adding to that stress.

Early one morning that week, Alle told me to call 911 because she felt like she was having a heart attack. She was literally in tears, and I asked her what she was feeling and why she was feeling that way. She had no answers, Alle said, because she had never experienced it before. But she then proceeded to tell me she was going to need ice cream, no, strawberry ice cream, while we waited.

So, instead of calling 911, I called her mom, who was a nurse. Her mom told me Alle wasn't having a heart attack. It was heartburn.

I was sweating.

I was laughing.

I was in shock.

I experienced a wide range of emotions in one hour due to Alle's heartburn.

And the pregnancy wasn't done scaring me.

At the last two appointments, the doctor shared that TJ's head was too large and that Alle's cervix might not be big enough for vaginal birth. If all went well with her dilating, the delivery would be fine, but we had to be prepared for a C-section.

Well, as you already know, we had to go with the C-section, and all went fine. But during TJ's first moments on Earth, I had my doubts that everything *was* fine. His head was shaped like a cone. He looked like retired NBA player Sam Cassell, whom some lovingly call "Alien," due to the shape of his head.

I had a freak-out moment. I pictured TJ growing up with a cone-shaped head, being mocked, and needing a special oval-shaped helmet if he followed in my footsteps and played football.

Of all the things to be concerned about . . . that was at the top of my list? I did not ask if his weight and size were okay. I did not ask if he had any neuromuscular disorders. I did not ask about his eyesight or hearing or anything like that. My only concern was the shape of his head.

As I stared at his head and gently stroked it, I asked if that was normal and if it would round out.

The doctor tried his best to not fall over laughing and to maintain a straight face in front of a first-time dad who assuredly had a mountain of fears building.

Yes, the doctor said, TJ's head would be fine. Baby heads are soft and are often misshaped for a variety of reasons while inside the womb. But in a short time, TJ's head would expand and become round.

The next day, I realized I had a lot of "errands" and would have to miss the circumcision. They were very important errands. Life-or-death errands . . . the most important errands I have ever had to run. They just so happened to all be scheduled at the exact moment that my baby's penis would be snipped.

As my bad luck would have it, I finished running my errands and made it back to the hospital just as the circumcision was complete. I just missed it . . . Talk about bad luck.

I was then handed my baby, and yes, the first thing I checked on was his head. It was nice and round, and he was long and handsome. And he had a head full of curly shiny black hair and bright brown eyes. He was perfect. I thanked God that the doctor was right. I also thanked God that TJ inherited his mother's hair.

———

I used to dress my sons the same.

Not exactly the same, as though they were twins and I was trying to test if friends and family could tell them apart, but I did dress them in similar fashions.

As the oldest, TJ set the standard. He established what he liked early on in his life, and then when Titus grew out of baby clothes, he inherited TJ's hand-me-downs. And when I purchased new clothes for Titus, they were from the same stores and sections as TJ's.

Then when Titus was around six or seven, he began dressing outrageously. When I would tell my sons to get dressed for dinner or a movie or a sporting event, TJ would come downstairs dressed to the nines, and Titus would strut to the door, wearing a striped shirt and plaid pants that clashed in both color and design.

I would demand he change. He would refuse. I would put down my fatherly foot. And he would change into clothes that looked like TJ's. But then, days later, he would dress again like a preppy clown. I would again tell him to change. He would again refuse. This went on for months.

Finally, I decided to stop putting my foot down and start listening.

I asked why he was determined to dress like a fool. And Titus explained it was because he did not like the clothes he had. He is not TJ, he said. He has his own fashion sense, his own identity.

The next day, Titus and I went clothes shopping.

I'm not a perfect father. No one is. Sometimes, a mistake is harmless, like dressing your son like his brother when he has a different style.

Other times, a mistake can be more serious.

My sons were probably eight and six on the day I took them with me to run errands, one of which included stopping by their aunt's house to leave something on her doorstep. I don't remember what exactly I was delivering to her, but I clearly recall what I forgot to do before I got out of the car and took a few steps to the door. I forgot to put the car in park. And my sons were still in it.

TJ started screaming for me. Maybe three seconds had elapsed before I heard him and registered what was happening. The car rolled maybe a few inches because it was stopped on a flat road. No harm, no foul, right?

I realize that it could have been worse. What if I had parked on a steep hill that day? What if something horrible had happened?

We all make mistakes. We all have lapses of judgment. But we cannot let such incidents paralyze us with fear.

For many, the world can seem like a scary place, made even scarier by the internet that can now diagnose our illnesses with a simple keyword search and have us believing we are dying of a rare fifth-century disease when we are actually just having an allergic reaction to a high pollen count.

I have never been the type of person who falls into internet rabbit holes that leave you shaking in your boots. But a lot of parents are that type, and I can understand why. Online searches can be terrifying.

You can learn the number of children who die each year from heatstroke, sometimes because their parents forget that they are in the car.

You can learn the number of children who drown each year, and how many of those drownings occur in a home pool.

You can learn the number of children who die each year from choking on food their parents have prepared.

You can learn the number of children who die each year from unintentional poisoning by ingesting household products.

You can learn the number of children who die each year when attacked by an alligator, a bear, or a woodpecker.

Worst yet, you can learn the number of children who die each year in mass shootings.

Many believe the world to be a dangerous place. And they can feel overwhelmed, wondering how they are supposed to keep their children safe.

Sure, we can childproof our homes, but we cannot childproof the world. So, then what?

We need parenting advice, so we again turn to the internet. But that advice can be contradictory.

One website says that we should always be attentive. But another recommends to not be too attentive. Neither explains where the line is.

One website says that we should not let our kids watch the news because that can teach them about violence. But another says that we cannot hide our kids from the truths of the real world.

One website says that we need to be friends with our children. Another says that we should always remain the parental figure.

One website says that we need to prioritize time with our partner. Another says that we need to prioritize time for ourselves.

It can be maddening, and it can turn you into a helicopter parent.

I have never been a fearful parent. I have always had faith in God and belief that the Almighty will look out for my family.

There are certainly times when I want to question parents who hover so closely over their children that they can swat away every germ that comes within a few feet of them. I want to tell them that they can protect their children through prayer, sound advice, and consistent conversation, but, at the end of the day, they cannot protect their children from everything. I want to tell those parents that no matter what they do, their kids are going to face challenges, get sick, and fall and bruise.

Before I get too preachy, I remember that with all the major problems kids face in this world, I was worried about the shape of my son's head. It was only a momentary concern, but nonetheless it was a concern.

We are all going to have our moments. The goal should be to limit those moments so that we can maintain a level head—a round one.

Hurricanes are a surreal part of life here in Florida.

One day, you're outside taking a long walk and enjoying the beautiful weather without a care in the world. The next day, the news tells you that death and destruction are on the way, and you are standing in lines at stores, zombie-eyed, trying to buy wood to board up your windows and enough water and toilet paper to survive nuclear fallout.

In 1992, I was 15 and living at the Boys Ranch when Hurricane Andrew ravaged South Florida. I was far from the eye of the storm and never in danger, but it's impossible to forget seeing the aftermath in newspapers and on television. Entire neighborhoods were leveled. Sturdy homes were turned inside out and became piles of splintering wood. Trees were uprooted. Water filled the streets. A lot of people died.

As a hurricane bares down on Florida, we all experience some form of fear. And then after it passes, unless it hits your town, life goes back to normal, but the visions of destruction always remain in the recesses of our minds.

It was August 2004. TJ was a little more than a month old, and we had just recently closed on our new home in Cape Coral. We had a 15-mile commute from our old apartment and our school jobs, and we were excited about having a home and a newborn. It had been overwhelming yet such a joy to hit so many milestones in such a short time. TJ was doing great. He had already graduated from his blue-light hospital incubator used to heal him from jaundice to sharing a bed with Alle and me in our two-bedroom apartment to having his own crib in his very own room. I cannot begin to explain how important it was for him to have his own room. When he shared a bed with us, I sometimes stayed awake worrying I would roll over and crush him. Plus, I never had my own room as a child. We couldn't afford an apartment that was big enough for the family, let alone a house. He was getting a beginning that I did not have.

We were so blessed to have friends and family donate the baby gear that all new parents need; these same folks also assisted us on the big move into our new home. It's always nice to be able to ask former and current football teammates to help load and unload a U-Haul. With Alle needing her rest due to the C-section and a newborn to care for, every helping hand was greatly appreciated. Especially in the middle of summer. It was hot.

We did not have much in our new place. The furniture from our apartment seemed so small there. But we had just what we needed to start out as a new family: our bed, TJ's crib, a small leather couch with an ottoman, and a floor television. It was a great start. We would eventually go to a couple of garage sales to find a dining set. A family friend donated a high chair for TJ.

As we continued to embrace our new roles, including sleepless nights and new schedules, we were also on high alert during hurricane season. In the second week of August, we began hearing that we needed to prepare for Hurricane Charley, which looked like it might be coming straight for us in the Cape. Thankfully, our new home came with hurricane shutters. But those shutters would only do so much if we were hit directly. And what if our home was spared but there was enough damage to our community to upend our lives—no food, no water, no gas. I can handle anything. But my son was still learning to hold up his own head. I did not want him to deal with any inconveniences.

Our greatest concerns were upon us as new parents and new homeowners, and I was faced with the age-old Florida hurricane question. As the Clash once sang, "Should I stay or should I go?" Do we stay at our new home, or do we seek refuge with family members who were not expecting the same weather we were preparing for? The question takes on greater importance when the life of a helpless baby is in your hands.

We eventually decided to stay and hunker down in our home. I purchased flashlights, candles, and other items in case we lost power. But I did not feel prepared. On the eve of Hurricane Charley, the shutters were up and our vehicles were in the garage. Everything we needed to do to prepare was done. The wait was all that was left.

The next morning, like almost everyone else in the Cape, Alle and I stared blankly at the television, listening to updates. One moment, we bit our lips as the eye of the hurricane was heading straight for us. The next moment, it shifted and was predicted to make landfall 30 miles away in Port Charlotte.

That is another one of those strange Florida hurricane feelings. You celebrate when you are spared, but you're also aware that means someone else's life will be shattered.

Ultimately, we avoided direct impact. However, our area and our home did take on damage from the 105 mile per hour winds. Our patio screens were bent in, some trees were leaning on both sides of our home and others were uprooted, and we went without power or water for days. I was thankful we were just inconvenienced, and I prayed for those who were not spared.

I then decided to drive my family over to my mother's home in Boynton Beach, Florida. Thankfully, we had that option.

That was such a stressful time for us. My family's health and well-being rested heavy on my shoulders. Then came the hurricane. Managing it all and keeping them safe during that time was my priority, and it was a huge responsibility. As I look back now and think about how it all turned out, I'm both amazed and grateful. That entire situation could have been really devastating for me as a husband and as a new father.

———

Of course I had dreams of playing professional football at the highest level.

I wasn't drafted out of the University of Florida, but I was invited to multiple training camps and chose the Jacksonville Jaguars. I seemed poised to make the team as a defensive end, until I tore my right ACL during a pass rush drill.

I was pretty certain my chance at playing in the NFL had all but disappeared. So I looked into high school coaching while continuing to rehab my knee, just in case a professional window ever opened again.

It did, but not for the NFL

I was offered a job with the Arena Football League's Las Vegas Gladiators, which I took. I later played for teams in Tampa and Utah.

Arena football paid well and provided insurance for my family. And even though it wasn't the NFL, it fulfilled my dream of playing professional football. But by then, football was more of a job than a passion. It was a way to support my family while I sought out a head coaching position.

Then the league began to change for the worse. Teams folded. Pay decreased. My final year as a professional football player was 2007. By then, my second son, Titus, was a year old.

I had two sons and lacked financial stability.

I will not say I was stressed. I rarely get overwhelmed by life. I came from meager beginnings, and my sons already had more than I ever did. While I wasn't stressed, I felt angst due to uncertainty.

I could not find a head coaching job. I considered returning to the University of Florida to work for the football program there, but there was no guarantee that would work out.

Then I sort of stumbled into a career with WWE. (I later stumbled into infamy with the Titus Slide at the *Greatest Royal Rumble* event. More on that later.) My best friend and brother Dave Bautista was already a WWE Superstar. He suggested I give it a try.

Quick aside: he *is* my brother, even if we are not linked biologically. We met while training at the same gym in Tampa and have since become the ying to the other's yang. He is a bit of an introvert and chooses to have a small select group of friends, while I am outgoing, an extrovert and consider most everyone to be a friend. He admittedly is not the smartest, most athletic, or best-looking guy around, while, well, I am. But we also have a lot in common. For instance, we are willing to outwork everyone and anyone. We both dare anyone to try to work harder than us. Since we met, we've grown from friends to best friends to brothers. We love one another like blood. We love one another's kids like blood. My kids never call him Dave or Bautista. He is always Uncle Bautista to them and always on the top of their invite list when deciding who to celebrate occasions with.

Now, back to our story.

In 2009, I popped into the WWE training facility that was in Tampa, introduced myself to Dusty Rhodes and Steve Keirn, who ran it, and a few weeks later I was training to become a WWE Superstar. A year later, I was on television.

Luckily, the angst of being a young father searching for a career path was short-lived, and there is no question my life is 10,000 times better because I have had the opportunity to work in WWE. Not only has it provided my family with a great income, but it has enabled me to travel the world and interact with people of all kinds. I probably could have played in the NFL for 10 years and not had a fraction of the worldly experiences that WWE has provided nor the opportunities to make as large an impact on the community.

But early on, being with WWE also added a parenting hurdle and more stress.

I had to learn to say no.

We're called WWE Superstars but we are also global super-stars, recognizable anywhere in the world. That recognition has allowed me to give back to others in ways I never imagined were possible.

I have been able to raise millions for charities, secure scholarships for hundreds of student athletes, and actively and financially support a school that's been named after me.

When you can help everyone, it can be hard to *not want to* help everyone. And when you have helped people countless times, sometimes it's hard for people to accept that you cannot help them.

So, when I was still a young father and new to WWE, I found myself agreeing to help, even when I knew I did not have the time to do it.

A teacher or a coach would ask that I come speak to a group of kids. I would want to help, but they would provide me with only 15 minutes to speak, the school or field would be 45 minutes away, and saying yes meant I would have a tight window to make it back across town to pick up my children from school or make it to one of their games.

Early on, I would say yes, always, and then stress in my car as I sat in traffic trying to make it back to my kids. That night, I would sit at home and wonder if it had been worth it. Had I really changed any lives in those 15 minutes? Or was I used as a photo opportunity?

I knew I had to prioritize better, but I felt guilty saying no. I never wanted to let anyone down, but in the process, I was letting myself down. I did not realize the mental toll it was taking. I needed counseling. I needed to unload my burden to someone. I needed to admit I was overwhelmed. But admitting that is taboo for a father.

New mothers often have a tremendous support system, and for good reason. As men, we will never understand the mental and physical toll it takes to grow a person inside your body and nurse them into this world. So women have hospital workers, counselors, their mother, grandmothers, and female friends who can help them through. They have maternity leave and time to adjust. They have a village.

While men might not have the same burden as women, we are burdened, nonetheless. We are expected to provide for the family while always being there for the mother and children.

Yes, it's no longer the 1800s. Women provide too, equally and more so in many instances. But there is still a societal stigma that men feel the need to be the primary provider while the children are young so that the mother can focus on them.

I don't think enough people talk about the pressure that fathers feel. Thus, fathers are embarrassed to talk openly about those pressures. Rather than having a village, we are alone on an island.

We are the last ones to eat dinner, the last ones to buy something for ourselves, the last ones to sit down and relax each night. We are determined to make sure that everyone in the house—mother and children—are okay each night before we check in to see if we are okay.

Fathers are not told to take care of their physical health. Fathers are not told to take care of their mental health. We are only conditioned to take care of everyone else.

We feel guilty when we are overwhelmed, fearful, or uncertain.

Yes, it might have been silly to worry about the shape of my son's head, but it was a concern, nonetheless. It might seem silly for a father to fall into an internet rabbit hole of fear, but it happens. Yes, most Floridians are fearful during a hurricane, but instead of talking about their feelings, many men internalize that fear and puff out their chests instead.

It wasn't until 2015 that I realized I was putting too much pressure on myself and sought out counseling.

I spoke with my pastor. I also spoke with a professional counselor.

They taught me it was okay to prioritize time for myself and it was okay to tell a teacher or coach I didn't have time to speak with a few children for a few minutes. They told me I had to realize that I did the best that I could.

Counseling remains taboo for men of my and older generations, especially among Black men. I think counseling makes men feel weak. Men want to portray machismo: they must be strong; they must be the backbone of the family; they must be a rock. Yada, yada, yada.

Getting counseling was a game changer for me. My pastor can tell me something from a spiritual perspective, but sometimes I need to hear it from the flawed human perspective.

A close friend may offer that perspective, but it's unlikely. Men primarily don't talk like that. We prefer to bond over beers and football rather than feelings and emotion, which is part of the problem.

I think counseling is beginning to become more acceptable among the younger generation of men who were raised in a society that, for the first time, said it was okay for men to seek help. But it still carries a stigma among that group and an even larger stigma among men my age and older who have a hard time accepting that times have changed.

My very first counseling session was eye-opening. My counselor stated that I had done a lot for a lot of people and raised millions of dollars for worthy causes. But then he asked if I felt overwhelmed, to which I replied that I sometimes did. He also asked if I had a problem saying no, which I said was indeed the case.

He told me there was a mental exercise that he wanted me to do. He asked me to close my eyes and imagine that I was the wealthiest person in the world and had the opportunity to use all my money to alleviate two global issues. What would those be, he asked. Hunger and homelessness, I said.

"Everybody in the world will have food and a place to live the moment I snap my fingers," the counselor said. He then counted to three and snapped his fingers. "Boom. Those problems are solved. Do you feel pride? Do you feel like you've given back to society?"

I nodded my head, but then came the lesson.

Kids are still dying of cancer, he said. Wars are still being fought. The environment is still being polluted, and so on.

"So, you just went flat broke solving two problems, but the world still has plenty more," the counselor said. "Hopefully, this illustrates that you cannot go broke trying to make everybody happy. You cannot go broke spiritually, mentally, physically, emotionally, and financially trying to accommodate everyone."

My mind was blown in that instant.

If you know of my work with the community, you are aware I still give back on a grand level. Every year, I make sure that tens of thousands of underprivileged kids have school supplies and Christmas presents. Throughout the year, I visit sick and at-risk kids in every city where WWE performs, and I take groups of kids to the movies, on trips, or even just for a meal.

I also now find time for myself. I no longer feel guilty for telling someone I can't help them on the exact day and time they need me because I already have plans to get a massage, meet friends for dinner, or go to a sporting event. I don't always have to be Superman.

And the counselor's lesson taught me a lot about parenting too. You cannot go broke trying to solve all your children's problems. You cannot fix everything. Being a parent is like a game of Whac-A-Mole. Another problem is always going to pop up. Just do your best and know it is good enough.

It's okay to admit you stay up late wondering if you are up for the task. It's okay to admit you wonder if you can be the financial and mental rock that your family needs you to be. It's okay to admit that, yes, you are paralyzed by an irrational fear that your newborn will drown, be left in the car, be eaten by an alligator, or have an odd-shaped head.

It's okay to fail. And it's okay to ask for help. New mothers need help. But so do new fathers.

You don't always have to be Superman. Sometimes it's okay to be Clark Kent. He's a heck of a guy.

CHAPTER 3

DON'T BE LIKE ME. BE BETTER THAN ME.

I n 2018, I raised enough money to take nearly 4,000 kids to see the first Black Panther movie.

All the kids were less fortunate. Most were Black.

Black Panther was, and remains, one of my favorite movies ever. Upon its release, the primary reason was that I thought it was important for Black men, women, and children to see themselves portrayed as superheroes on a big screen. Years later, I have a secondary but just as important reason.

I now realize that, at its heart, *Black Panther* is a movie about father-son relationships, and it's one that is in line with my parental philosophy.

I tell my kids all the time: "Don't be like me. Be better than me."

For that to happen, it starts with my actions.

Parents sometimes tell their children to do one thing while they themselves do the complete opposite, which can be confusing to their kids. If I tell my children to respect and love other people, but then turn around and disrespect others, how can I expect my kids to follow my rule? I'm their first role model and, regardless of my social status, whether I'm a WWE Superstar or unemployed, I want to be the one my kids want to emulate. But I also need my children to know that I'm not perfect and that they should not emulate my flaws.

In *Black Panther*, T'Challa's wisdom, grace, and warrior mentality were taught to him by his father, King T'Chaka. King T'Chaka says to T'Challa, "A man who has not prepared his children for his death has failed as a father." But King T'Chaka had flaws too.

He had kept a secret. He had killed his own brother and orphaned his nephew. And he did that because he was too nationalistic, preferring to keep Wakanda's riches for Wakanda, rather than using them to uplift other nations.

After his father died, T'Challa had to deal with the fallout from those mistakes. Rather than doubling down, refusing to admit his father wasn't perfect and then following in Dad's footsteps, T'Challa sought to correct those mistakes.

"No man is perfect, not even your father," Nakia, a fellow warrior, tells T'Challa. "You cannot let your father's mistake define who you are."

Or, as I like to say, "Don't be like me. Be better than me."

———

"Don't be like me, be better than me" should apply to all families. Even those with parents who reached extraordinary heights. If a mother or a father has climbed the highest mountain, their children should want to fly to the moon, and the parents should support that dream.

My good friend, the well-decorated, award-winning, billion-dollar-box-office movie producer Will Packer, often tells the story of his first day in his St. Petersburg, Florida, middle school gifted program. Even before he stepped foot in the classroom, he was angry about being moved into the program because it meant leaving his friends behind. He did not know anyone in the new class.

Once Will entered the classroom, he felt he was an outcast. He was the only Black student. He went home that day and pleaded with his parents to let him return to his former class. "I don't want to be gifted," Will told them. "I don't want to stand out."

His parents let him finish his rant, explained that they understood why he felt that way, but then made it clear he was in that program for good. By staying, he could perhaps influence his fellow students, who might have preconceived notions about Black people.

"All eyes are on you, and that's a good thing," Will's father told him. "Show them who you are. Show them who we are. Use your race to your advantage. The other kids have to do something to stand out. You already stand out. So now, what you do with that attention and this opportunity is what matters."

The 2022 Academy Awards will be remembered by historians as the pinnacle for Will. It marked the first time that the Oscars were produced by an all-Black production team. They were fittingly led by Will Packer, who just six years earlier was among the most vocal to point out that the Academy Awards had a diversity problem; his film, the NWA biopic *Straight Outta Compton*, was considered one of the most obviously snubbed Black-made films that year.

It was a big moment for an industry that had historically been dominated by white producers. The only asterisk on that night was when Will Smith slapped Chris Rock—but I believe Will Packer's accomplishment, in time, will be what we remember most about that evening.

Over the years, many helped my friend Will Packer ascend to that height in his career.

But perhaps no one better prepared him for it than his father, Will Packer Sr., the St. Petersburg civil rights icon who was the first Black student to graduate from the University of South Florida engineering school, chaired the St. Petersburg Martin Luther King Jr. Commemorative Commission, and mentored countless young Black men and women during that era of struggle.

His father would sometimes give Will short yet powerful lectures, often repeating his mantra, "You can play now and pay later, or you can pay now and play later." But he primarily led by example.

As a kid, Will did not realize that his father was an important figure. For Will, his dad was just his dad. He knew that his dad was often at meetings that were considered important. He knew that his dad was always on the forefront of the local mission to honor Dr. King. He knew that young Black men and women often congregated at his house on weekends. He knew that little Black kids would often surround his father at the nearby community center to listen to his advice. Yet, to Will, he remained the man at whom he would get angry when his allowance was docked as punishment.

Will did not realize his father's standing until high school. He went with his father to a Dr. King event. There, Will witnessed St. Petersburg's mayor fawning over his father. The mayor then looked to Will and said, "You must be so proud to have this man as your father." That night, Will rewound his childhood in his mind and realized his dad was more than his dad. It was the first time he appreciated what his father meant to the community.

Still, as Will tells it, looking back, his father had already had a major influence over him just by silently being a good role model. His father's drive, entrepreneurship, and philanthropic heart had rubbed off on him. By high school, Will already knew he wanted to be successful so he could inspire others to succeed in their own way.

Will is absolutely self-made. After graduating from Florida A&M University in 1996, he knew that it was difficult to break into Hollywood, and even more difficult for a Black man. So, four years later, rather than hoping Hollywood would accept his first movie, the erotic thriller *Trois*, he took matters into his own hands, barnstorming like he was on the old Chitlin, Circuit.

Will cut deals with 20 movie theaters in Black communities throughout the nation, and his movie's opening weekend was second, per screen, to only Disney's *Fantasia 2000*. The film eventually made more than $1 million, making it one of the top 50 highest grossing independent productions of the year.

From there, he went on to produce movies such as *Stomp the Yard*, *Ride Along*, and *Almost Christmas*. As I write this, his more than three dozen movies have grossed over $1 billion. I would like to write that after the success of *Trois*, he never looked back. But he did, often and in a good way.

His father died in 2008, but Will often thought of him whenever he faced an obstacle or great task, including those 2022 Oscars.

The good and bad thing about being the first to do something, Will likes to say, is that you are the first. Years later, it sounds great to say you were the first to accomplish something, but it can be a lonely journey while doing so. There is no fraternity of past success stories to provide advice or inspiration. It can take an extreme amount of confidence to believe that you can not only break a glass ceiling but do so in a way that shines a positive light on the accomplishment. When first at anything, it's no different than Will's middle school gifted program: all eyes are on you.

So, in spirit, Will's father provided him with the strength to lead that first all-Black Academy Awards production team. He recalled his father's fearlessness. And when he realized that the Oscars were equivalent to producing 10 major Hollywood movies, he recalled his father's mantra: "You can play now and pay later, or pay now and play later."

"Everybody is not fortunate enough to have parents that are genuinely great role models, genuinely doing things that one would aspire to," Will once told me. "I am so fortunate and blessed that my father was not only a great man to aspire to be and not only a role model for me, but a role model for the community."

Will's father was a role model for St. Petersburg. Will became a role model for the entire world.

"Don't be like me, be better than me."

———

We can admit it. As parents, we blush when someone tells us our kids look just like us.

There is even a secret competition between spouses over whose DNA is dominant within the children. My children have the best of both worlds from both their mother and father, though I do often wonder from whom they get their handsome good looks. No, actually, I don't.

"Beauty is only skin deep" is one of the truest statements of all time. I have met plenty of people who were gorgeous on the outside but hideous on the inside.

I like to think that deep down, beauty comes from one's parents, and how a mother and father treat others directly influences how their children treat others. If you treat people with respect, there is a pretty good chance your children will do so too. Whether you come from a privileged background or from a simple one, it's important to remember we are all human beings, regardless of social status, socioeconomic status, race, creed, or gender. How we treat others and how we teach our kids to treat others will be a great signal to the world that humanity is still alive and well.

I realized early on how much a parent can influence a child.

Again, I'm afraid of needles, afraid to the point that I even squirm when watching others receive injections. I still don't know how I made it through TJ's delivery when doctors injected giant needles into Alle's stomach; I sometimes compare it to when someone can lift a car off their children. A rush of adrenaline helped me make it through those needles.

And guess what? My sons are afraid of needles too.

Perhaps they would have been afraid anyway.

Or perhaps, even as babies, they sensed that I was closing my eyes and clenching my jaw as they received vaccinations or gave blood.

Our kids mimic what they see.

———

I'm a WWE Superstar and Global Ambassador for several reasons, one of which is because of the initial encouragement from David Bautista to consider sports entertainment as a career. Another big reason is my sons.

After visiting the WWE's training facility in Tampa and being offered the opportunity to learn there, I took my sons to an FCW show—a precursor to today's NXT. As we watched fellow behemoths kick, punch, and slam one another, I turned to my sons and asked if they thought I could do that.

Titus replied, "It'd be cool," and TJ said, "I think you can do anything, Daddy."

They both then agreed to become my biggest fans.

They lived up to their word and have always been the unofficial president and vice president of the Titus O'Neil Fan Club. I will let them fight it out for who has the higher of the two positions.

Over the years, no matter how WWE has booked my character, Titus O'Neil has had one constant: as I enter the ring, I look into the hard camera and throw up the hooks representing my Omega Psi Phi Fraternity, Inc.

A year or so after I began training with WWE, my sons watched me perform in the ring. The next day while at home, Titus came down the stairs wearing a University of Florida football jersey that was so big on him it was more like a dress, and I thought he would trip on it and stumble to the floor. He made it to the bottom of the stairs, screamed, "Look at me, Daddy," and then showed me the hooks.

Our kids mimic what they see.

———

I have twice been nominated for ESPN's Muhammad Ali Sports Humanitarian Award, which, according to the sports network, is "given annually to an athlete whose continuous, demonstrated leadership has created a measured positive impact on their community through sports. The candidate must embrace the core principles that Muhammad Ali embodied, including confidence, conviction, dedication, giving, and respect."

I have twice been nominated and twice lost. Do I wish I had won? Well . . .

Just being nominated is a high accomplishment, being nominated twice even more so—very few people, if any, have ever been.

If you are giving back only for the attention that it brings, then you are actually a selfish person rather than a giving one. When I look at the work I do, it's never about striving for accolades and awards, but rather about doing what God has positioned me to do. I sometimes consider people who are "giving back" yet seeking attention and pats on the back for doing so as selfish. One cannot determine their success in giving back based on how many accolades they have received. I'm at a point in my life where I understand that the significance of my work outweighs the accolades.

But, ultimately, a small part of me wishes I had won. I'm human after all.

Muhammad Ali really was the greatest: he was the greatest to ever slip on a pair of boxing gloves and joust in that ring. And along with Jim Brown, Kareem Abdul-Jabbar, Walter Payton, and Magic Johnson, he was among the greatest athletes for the work he did for the community.

Ali was never afraid of a fight, either with another boxer or with what he perceived to be an evil in our society. I have lived my life trying to emulate him, and it's humbling to be compared to the man who could float like a butterfly and sting like a bee.

But I'm even prouder when people compare me to my dad, Mr. Blalock.

We don't share a drop of DNA. Physically, we look nothing alike. Yet when I look in the mirror, I proudly see my dad looking back.

When I look at my sons, I sometimes see myself and sometimes see my dad. It might be the little things, like the cadence in their voices, that reminds me of my dad. Other times, our sense of humor is like my dad's.

Not one of us has ever tripped and fell without another one of us, sometimes a few of us in unison, shouting sarcastic remarks: "Have a nice trip?" or "I thought it was summer, not fall." While we are empathetic and sympathetic to others, we don't have a problem laughing at ourselves. Lovingly poking fun at family is part of being a family, or at least a part of being my family.

And then there are times when I don't see Mr. Blalock—on those occasions, I sometimes see his father, my grandfather.

Before I explain, a history lesson is necessary.

Black men throughout the South were freed from enslavement and granted "equal rights" the moment the Confederate Army submitted to the Union Army. But we all know that while the Southerners removed the physical shackles from the enslaved, they remained in figurative chains. The 15th Amendment was supposed to guarantee the right to vote for all Black men, but white Southerners found ways to "legally" continue to stop them from fulfilling the greatest civic duty bestowed upon those living in a democracy.

The inhabitants of Florida were among the biggest perpetrators.

There were poll taxes that Black adults could not afford on their low wages. There were literacy tests at polls in communities that did not provide proper schooling for the Black community, if they received any education at all.

Another popular form of voter suppression was the white primary system. For years, there was no law against a political party forbidding Black voters from joining. So a community would demand that all white politicians register with the all-white party, making that primary the de facto general election.

And when all else failed, there was violence.

My dad was the eighth of nine children raised in the Florida town of Perry, known for its violent past. In 1922, a white woman was so brutally murdered there that police struggled to identify her.

But they quickly identified her killer as a Black man named Charley Wright.

Maybe he did it.

Maybe he did not.

He never received a trial in a court of law.

Instead, after he was arrested and while being transported to jail to await a fair trial, as many as 5,000 white men accosted and tried him in a kangaroo court. Without any evidence being presented, without an attorney or a judge present, they declared him guilty and burned him to death.

But that wasn't enough for the residents of Perry.

Days earlier, another Black man was shot to death as the search for Wright was underway. Deputized residents claimed that the man had reached for a gun.

He did not have a gun.

Days after Wright was murdered, another mob took his alleged accomplice from jail and shot him to death.

A few days later, another Black man, who did not have any ties to the Wright case, was shot to death and had his home burned because he had allegedly written an unacceptable letter to a white woman.

A white mob then decided to burn the Black community's school, church, and a few other important buildings.

Decades later, in 1951, the entire state of Florida was put on notice. The state's National Association for the Advancement of Colored People (NAACP) president, Harry T. Moore, was murdered on Christmas Day when someone detonated a bomb at his Miami home. Many believe this was done to suppress voting and the civil rights movement.

Now, back to my grandfather, also named Charles Blalock.

He was a hardworking man who spent much of his adult life employed at a sawmill and later a paper factory. That second job paid well for those times, especially for a Black man, but not enough for such a large family to live comfortably. But the kids never knew they were poor. That was just life for them.

He was strict, yet fun.

Saturdays were for play. The kids were told to go outside and play until they dropped. But Sundays were for God. They would arrive at church at 11 a.m. and remain there through the evening.

The kids knew better than to cross their dad.

My father tells a funny story about blackmailing his sisters. On some Saturdays, my grandfather gave 15 cents to each of his kids to go to the movies. Admission was a nickel, popcorn another nickel, and a soda yet another. Well, when my dad's sisters had dates whom they allowed to get a bit frisky, he would walk up to them, palm extended, and demand one of their nickels as payment to remain silent. They would quickly pay up. Losing out on a soda or popcorn was a better option than facing their father.

Knowing the history of racism, violence, and voter suppression, no one would have blamed my grandfather for focusing on being a father and nothing else. No one would have blamed him for staying out of the civil rights movement.

But he wasn't made that way.

Instead, in the face of such racism, he sought to lead.

He was one of the first Black residents of Perry to exercise his right to vote. My dad was 10 or 11 at the time that my grandfather voted, which was also around the time that the state's NAACP president was murdered.

Apparently, nothing would deter my grandfather. He then formed a Black Voters League in Perry to encourage others to vote. Through this organization, he became such a force that candidates, even those running for governor, visited him for an endorsement, knowing it would help them to win Perry's Black vote.

Years later, at the age of 71 or 72, my grandfather traveled regularly to the state's capital of Tallahassee to serve as Florida's oldest legislative page. That is a job historically filled by high school students, but my grandfather took it because he so wanted to be a part of the legislative process.

"Don't be like me. Be better than me."

That is what my father sought to do by adopting his father's attitude and pushing even more for the betterment of the Black community.

My dad is a civil rights icon in Florida. He was the first Black person to ever serve as a principal in Hamilton County and was then later elected the first Black superintendent in both Suwannee and Hamilton Counties, defeating white candidates in areas where the white population neared 90 percent.

One of my favorite stories about my dad was the time that a white man offered him a campaign contribution with the caveat that it was their secret. My dad refused, matter-of-factly explaining that he would never accept support from anyone who would not do so publicly.

My dad always had advice for me, often first reciting Rudyard Kipling's poem "If," which embodied much of what he stood for.

If you can keep your head when all about you
Are losing theirs and blaming it on you;
If you can trust yourself when all men doubt you,
But make allowance for their doubting too;
If you can wait and not be tired by waiting,
Or, being lied about, don't deal in lies,
Or, being hated, don't give way to hating,
And yet don't look too good, nor talk too wise;

If you can dream—and not make dreams your master;
If you can think—and not make thoughts your aim;
If you can meet with Triumph and Disaster

And treat those two impostors just the same;
If you can bear to hear the truth you've spoken
Twisted by knaves to make a trap for fools,
Or watch the things you gave your life to broken,
And stoop and build 'em up with worn out tools;

If you can make one heap of all your winnings
And risk it on one turn of pitch-and-toss,
And lose, and start again at your beginnings
And never breathe a word about your loss;
If you can force your heart and nerve and sinew
To serve your turn long after they are gone,
And so hold on when there is nothing in you
Except the Will which says to them: "Hold on!";

If you can talk with crowds and keep your virtue,
Or walk with kings—nor lose the common touch;
If neither foes nor loving friends can hurt you;
If all men count with you, but none too much;
If you can fill the unforgiving minute
With sixty seconds' worth of distance run
Yours is the Earth and everything that is in it,
And—which is more—you will be a Man, my son!

This poem is written as though a father is dispelling advice to a son. It reminds us to remain calm while others panic, to avoid lying when being lied to, to not become trapped by our ambitions, to never hate even when hated.

My dad's favorite lesson from the poem is to be strong enough to lose everything and start from scratch again.

But I often look to the final stanza: "If you can fill the unforgiving minute with sixty seconds' worth of distance run."

Even though I was elected vice president of the University of South Florida's student body, I have never had real political ambitions, unlike my grandfather and father. But I have sought to better the world in other ways—by filling every second of the unforgiving minute with acts of kindness.

And just as my grandfather influenced my father who influenced me to serve the community, I can see my influence on my sons.

During my sophomore year of high school, I befriended a homeless man who often hung outside our football practices. I brought him food. Upon learning he was once a CEO of a Fortune 500 company but lost everything because of drugs, I helped him get work at a friend's family's car dealership. That man later turned his life around and moved into upper management with the company. From the time they could first understand the tales I told, I shared that story with my sons as an example of why they should always look out for others.

When Titus was six years old, we lost him at a store. As we frantically looked, TJ calmly pointed to where Titus was. He was in the back of the store, praying with a total stranger. The stranger then walked away with a friendly wave to us. "Why did you pray for that man?" we asked. He replied, "He seemed like he was hurting."

While in San Diego for a WWE event in 2015, I offered to buy a homeless man dinner. I walked him to a restaurant, handed the manager money, told him to sit the homeless man at a table and serve whatever he wanted, and went on my way. I later learned the restaurant refused to sit him and would only give the food to go. So I returned to the same restaurant the next day with 30 homeless people and sat with them to ensure each was fed at a table.

That received national attention, and weeks later, while in Los Angeles for *SummerSlam*, my sons and I were walking back to our hotel after dining out. TJ had barely touched his food, taking nearly an entire meal with him in a to-go container. As we passed a homeless man, as though second nature, TJ handed him the leftovers.

In 2018, prior to an *NXT Takeover* event, I met a fan who wanted to gift tickets to her boyfriend but could not afford the price, so I handed her $100 to make it happen.

That received national attention, and the following Christmas, while we were walking into a Walmart in Tampa, Titus noticed a family standing on the corner with their patriarch, who was playing the accordion, hoping for money. Well, Titus had $100 he had been given by a relative to buy a Christmas present for himself. Instead, Titus handed the money to that father.

There are only a few things, perhaps nothing, that I hate more than bullying. Even when I was a kid, I defended the bullied. If I was ever in a fight, it was with a bully.

As an adult, I have embraced WWE's Be a STAR anti-bullying campaign, which meets with kids in cities we visit and encourages the children to be respectful and tolerant and push back against bullying. Over and over, I have told my sons that bullying is a line that they should not cross. I will not tolerate raising a bully nor someone who doesn't stand up to bullies.

When TJ was around 10 years old, he witnessed a bully picking on a scrawny kid while at summer camp. TJ wasn't as big as the bully, but he did not care. Later, I received a call that

TJ had been in a fight at camp. I don't condone fighting, so I drove over there, ready to raise some hell. But in front of the camp leaders, TJ explained that he was defending a bullying victim, so I shook his hand and informed the other adults that I would not be punishing my son for his actions.

My sons embraced my best attitudes at a very young age, and both are on a path to exceed everything I have accomplished.

They are on their way to being not "like me" but "better than me."

———

In July 2022, when my dad visited Tampa, he came with me to Raymond James Stadium as I prepared for that year's Back to School Bash, which provides school supplies to the less fortunate.

Out of nowhere that day, he placed his hand on my shoulder and said, "Son, I know where you were heading. I know how you were supposed to grow up. You were a young man who wasn't supposed to graduate high school or college. And here you are doing something great with your life. I'm so proud of you."

I will never forget his words. Even as a grown man with grown children, a dream career, and the ability to touch the lives of countless men, women, and children around the world, I still need to hear from my parents that they are proud of me. In turn, I'm proud that they are my parents.

My kids are proud I'm their dad and proud of our family as a whole. When they talk about me, their mother, grandparents, and other family members, they light up. They are proud that their father is a global WWE Superstar, but, like my dad, they are prouder that I seek to do great things with that celebrity. People approach my sons about seeing me on television but approach them more so about something good I did for the community.

Because they are proud, they are less likely to act out in public or do something I might look down upon. They don't want to do anything that would not make me proud.

But that must be a two-way street. It must be. As parents, we should only act in ways that make our kids proud.

This is worth repeating: as parents, we are our sons' and daughters' first role models. It's from us that they first observe what a good human being and a good leader should be like, or at least what they think a good human being and a good leader should be like

No one can guarantee that you will always be able to be the best provider. Life happens. Things happen that are out of our control and could impact your ability to earn a living.

But you can always control the type of role model that you are. You can always be a person of character. You can always be a person who shows and exhibits compassion. You can always be a person whom other people admire, not necessarily because of what you do for a living but rather because of who you are.

I have found that the key to being a good role model to my kids is to act in ways that they would be proud to tell others.

Would they be proud to tell their friends that I got a DUI?

Would they be proud to tell their friends that I bully other people?

Would they be proud that I missed their football game because I went to a club instead?

Just as you seek to make your parents proud no matter your age, always seek to make your children proud too, and they will grow into the type of men and women of whom you are proud.

My maternal grandmother was the best chef in the history of my family—other than me, of course.

She owned a soul food bar just outside Delray Beach, where she cooked all the delicious staples. My mouth still waters when I think of her chicken.

My mother makes the best sweet potato pie in the world. But she did not inherit her mom's culinary skills. Most everything else she cooks is okay. I love my mother and respect her as much as I respect any human being ever, but, without an apology, I'm a better cook.

She may have had potential, but as a young mother, she never had the opportunity to cook anything gourmet. We did not have enough money for anything like that. We could not afford for her to experiment with making jerk or curry sauces or to discover the best way to prepare a prime rib. We primarily survived off food stamps that could purchase such "delicacies" as egg noodles and neck bones. But to her credit, my mother could open the refrigerator and cupboard and make a meal out of whatever was in there, even if the ingredients did not seem to mesh in any way. I will not say those meals were delicious, but they were palatable.

One thing my mother did inherit from her mother was the ability to bring people together with food.

Pretty much everyone in my neighborhood was in the same financial situation as we were. This meant that holidays, both federal and religious, were different around our way. Whereas in much of America, people gather with financial ease for barbecues on the Fourth of July or giant turkeys with all the sides for Thanksgiving, such festive meals were a struggle in my community.

My mother was often the one who sought to combat that struggle.

She would collect food stamps from friends for a trip to the store and ingredients from others, and then work her magic to make a neighborhood-wide meal. And those neighborhood gatherings are some of my fondest childhood memories: kids scattered about playing the sport of the day while comradery and a good meal allowed the adults to forget about their problems, if only for a bit.

I inherited my mother's penchant for bringing people together with food. Among my family and friends, I'm the one who hosts dinners or barbecues and plans gatherings at restaurants.

And I inherited my grandmother's culinary skills and then exceeded her.

"Don't be like me. Be better than me."

Traveling the world with WWE has allowed me to meet some of the planet's finest chefs, and my celebrity means those same chefs are more likely to share their culinary secrets and recipes with me.

I'm now confident I can cook just about anything.

My sons? Well, they might have inherited my joy of giving at an early age, but I have yet to find a way to get them interested in cooking. But there's time. And if they never show interest, hopefully I will have grandchildren on to whom I can pass my knowledge.

My mother passed something else on to me: anger.

She was an angry mother and had every right to be.

She wasn't even a teenager when I was born. She was then disowned by her family for choosing against having an abortion. Just a kid, she had to figure out how to afford and raise a kid on her own. On top of that, she had the anger that comes with being a rape survivor.

Her parenting style was to scream first, dole out a whooping second, and to never ask questions.

I inherited her anger and would scream back. The way we fought, we were more like siblings than mother and son.

I brought that anger with me to school. I yelled at teachers, and while I never fought anyone but bullies, I'm sure there were times when I could have found a peaceful solution had I not been so fueled by anger.

When I was a teen, my dad, other mentors, and the Boys Ranch taught me to tame that anger. My mother received the mental health counseling that she needed too. The Bullard family anger seemed behind us, or so I thought.

As a young father of two, I thought discipline meant yelling. Bad grades? I yelled. Forgot to do a chore? I yelled. Whatever the issue, I yelled.

And then when both my sons graduated from little boys into teenage young men, they both approached me about my yelling. They didn't like it, they said. It was unnecessary, they said. It bothered them and sometimes scared them, they said.

I'm a big man. But at that moment, I felt very tiny when I saw the earnest looks in their eyes. I took a breath and promised I would never again lose my cool with them.

I have kept my word.

And I hope that means I have broken the cycle. I hope it means they will never raise their voices in such a way toward their children.

"Don't be like me. Be better than me."

CHAPTER 4

DIVORCE

E ven though this is not a book about sports entertainment, for those who still hope to read stories about WWE, I figured I would throw you a bone. Or perhaps it's more apropos to throw you a bouquet (channeling my inner Dusty Rhodes), if you will.

So, let's talk about WWE marriages—not real-life marriages between WWE Superstars, but rather those scripted affairs that have long been a time-honored WWE television tradition.

Whenever WWE announces a televised wedding, the WWE Universe know that something crazy is going to happen.

Three such matrimonies stand out to me.

The first is the actual first wedding that WWE ever held. In 1985, Uncle Elmer wed Joyce Stazko on an episode of *Saturday Night's Main Event*. It was classic cartoonish 1980s WWE. The ring was filled with farm animals. Guests included Hillbilly Jim in his overalls and Hulk Hogan in a sleeveless shirt. Jesse "The Body" Ventura treated his color commentator duties like he was at a dais during a celebrity roast, and, of course, Rowdy

Roddy Piper, the ultimate bad guy at the time, had to interrupt to cut a schoolyard bully promo. The couple was successfully hitched. But something had to go wrong. During the reception, also televised, Ventura gave a speech that guests felt crossed the line, so Hillbilly Jim threw him into the cake.

Perhaps the most beloved WWE wedding was the one dubbed "The Match Made in Heaven" between "Macho Man" Randy Savage and "The First Lady of Wrestling" Miss Elizabeth. Their two characters had split up, with Savage joining forces with evil Sensational Sherri. But they got back together at the 1991 *Royal Rumble* when, in a match with his career on the line, Savage lost to the Ultimate Warrior. Sensational Sherri then turned against Savage, and Miss Elizabeth came to his rescue from out of the crowd, who went crazy for the reunion. In June of that year, Savage proposed to her on an episode of *Superstars of Wrestling*, with Miss Elizabeth replying, in her best Savage voice, "Oh yeah." And that was how Savage later said yes in August at their *SummerSlam* wedding. But, once again, things went badly at the reception. Jake "The Snake" Roberts's cobra leapt from a wedding present, and Undertaker used the distraction to hit Savage from behind with an urn.

And the most nefarious consequential wedding was, of course, the scripted nuptials of Triple H and Stephanie McMahon. Vince's little angel was set to marry Test on the November 29, 1999, episode of *Raw*. All was going well, until the priest proclaimed that if someone was against the wedding, "they must speak now or forever hold their peace." In the history of television and movie weddings, nothing good has ever followed that line. Triple H interrupted with a video that showed him marrying a passed-out Stephanie at a Las Vegas drive-through chapel. But at that year's *Armageddon* event, Stephanie turned on her father to help Triple H defeat him. She later admitted she was in on the wedding plan, doing so to exact revenge on her father for his past indiscretions. The McMahon-Helmsley era was then kicked off and ruled storylines for years to come, ruining the scripted lives of other WWE Superstars.

These three storylines made for great television, because we all love a wedding.

But no one loves a divorce. It's a topic we try to avoid, even after a split. For most, it's best to suppress the feelings that come with a divorce and just move on.

But when you have kids, you can't just move on from a divorce or your former spouse. You are tied to your ex for life. You are also tied to that divorce until your children become adults.

It's an uncomfortable reality to accept, but it is a reality. My marriage with my sons' mother lasted nine years, though we both knew a few years earlier that our happily ever after would not be an "ever after."

I'm not a proponent of divorce. I'm a proponent of marriage. But I'm not a proponent of bad marriage. And our marriage became bad.

We tried to save it. We went to counseling and did everything that the experts advised. We considered staying together for the kids. We wanted them to have a two-parent household, which neither of us had. We wanted to become that perfect sitcom family.

But we just could not right the ship. Our self-made storms kept rocking our marital boat off course. So we did what we both believed was the brave decision: we divorced. It takes a lot of courage to admit to the world that your marriage has failed. Staying together is not easier, but it's easier on your ego.

We were once very much in love. When we said "I do" and promised to love and cherish one another for better, for worse, for richer, for poorer, in sickness and in health, we meant every word of it. We truly believed we would be together for life and in the afterlife.

But life is not a sitcom. Sometimes, we must wake up from our warm dreams and face the cold reality.

Nothing ugly caused the rift. Neither drugs nor drinking caused our divorce. No one was abused mentally or physically. Neither of us was unfaithful.

Divorce doesn't always mean you or your partner is a bad person.

Life happens to all of us. People change. Some couples can deal with that change, and some grow apart.

We grew apart and nothing was going to bring us back together. Sometimes, two people can love one another but not be in love. And not being in love will ultimately create a divide in the home, a divide in the friendship, a divide in the pairing.

While at the time I did not think divorce was the right decision, years later I realized it was the best thing to happen for us both. We were not going to make one another the best versions of ourselves. My life is much different now and I see things very differently. Yes, I have had various relationships since my divorce, but I also know that, as a man, I'm in a better place now than I was when married to Alle, and she would say the same about herself.

During our divorce process, I leaned heavily on my pastor Gregory Powe Sr., my dad Mr. Blalock, and my best friend Ricky Sailor, and they were there for me every moment I needed them. I was never alone. Titus O'Neil is scripted to be a colorful, fun-loving tough guy who doesn't let anything get to him, not even a punch squarely to the jaw. But, again, I'm not Titus O'Neil. I'm Thaddeus Bullard, and I'm human—not indestructible.

Circumstances made my divorce a little easier than others.

For starters, my sons were both too young to realize anything was changing or to hold on to memories from that time in their lives.

And I had an easier time adjusting to what other fathers have told me is the most difficult part of a divorce: learning to be away from your children. My divorce occurred before I became a WWE Superstar, but just after my professional football playing days had ended. The travel schedule that came with playing in the Arena Football League prepared me for being away from my sons a few days a week. So being separated from them due to divorce did not feel too different. I was used to sleeping in a bed in one place while my sons slept elsewhere. And despite our differences, my ex-wife never kept them off the phone if I called to say goodnight, tell them that I loved them, or ask about their days.

My ex-wife and I never weaponized the kids against one another. I know divorced parents who air their dirty laundry in front of the kids, in hopes that saying something bad about their ex-spouse will turn the children against the ex and in their favor. I had plenty of things I could have said about my ex, and I'm certain she had plenty to say about me. Nothing major, just those small things that annoy you about an ex right after a relationship ends. But they might have seemed major to the kids and impacted how they looked at us.

Alle and I have also never been interested in getting into a parental competition. If I take my children to a concert, she doesn't feel compelled to take them to a movie the next day, and vice versa. If she plans something simple with my sons, I don't suddenly offer them a more exciting option for that same day, and vice versa. I have the means to do a lot of amazing things with and for my sons, but I would never do anything for them just to make her feel less than. I would never give my sons a spite gift. I can be petty, but I'm not that petty, especially when it comes to my family, and Alle, though we are divorced, is still part of my family. She is the mother of my children.

Divorce, if anything, emboldened me to be an even better father than I previously planned on being.

I wanted to break a family cycle.

My maternal grandfather left my grandmother before my mother was born, so she grew up without a father. Years later, when he tried to connect with me as I became a nationally known high school player during the college recruiting process, I learned that he had a respectful career through rental properties and by selling trees to lumberyards. And that he gave enough money to charities that he became a beloved man in his community. But he abandoned his child. That made him a loser. We spent time together, but I refused to let him become a big part of my life. I cannot respect an absentee father, and I cannot love a man whom I don't respect.

Again, I never met nor wanted to know the man who raped my mother.

My mother had my three brothers with Clifford, but he walked out on us after my youngest brother was born. So I never looked up to nor got along with him. I felt like he disrespected my mother, never treated me like a son, and did not live up to his fatherly obligations for my brothers.

Divorce has a way of separating fathers from their children.

I hear about it too often from kids I mentor. Some have a father who feel that the best way to deal with a divorce is to get as far away from his ex-wife as possible, even moving to the other side of the country to start over.

Others have mothers who, out of spite, do their best to cut the father out of their lives.

Then the little kids grow up wondering why Daddy is not at their games or Cub Scout meetings or birthday parties or holidays. The truth is, their mother or father is selfish, but that is a hard fact for a child to accept. In the minds of so many little kids, their parents are perfect. So if their father is absentee, the kids feel it's their fault, that they are not loveable.

I wasn't going to be that father.

No matter how hard it might have been to form a co-parenting relationship with my ex during those early post-divorce years, I had to do it. No, I wanted to do it. I did not want to miss a single one of my children's games or activities, so I wasn't going to let my strained relationship with their mother keep me away. I wasn't going to avoid them because I wanted to avoid her. Their mother was the same way. And I don't recall a single time when either of my sons asked where she was or my former wife telling me they had asked where I was. We were divorced, but we were still full-time parents to our sons.

But we were not a perfect divorced couple.

For years, we split the holidays. She got them Christmas, Easter, and Thanksgiving morning, and I got them in the afternoon, or vice versa. They went trick-or-treating with one of us and then went out with the other. They had two birthday parties. My ex and I were fine with it. We thought they were too.

Then in 2019, we learned otherwise. They told us it was important to have a Thanksgiving dinner where both parents were at the table together. Neither Alle nor I wavered for a moment when asked separately. We both immediately said yes. If it was important to them, it was important to us. My only request was that I host it. Alle is a great mother. But she is not a better chef than I am. My sons were so happy that day, and I truly believe it was one of the best decisions I have made as a father.

I want my kids to see that divorce does not mean a relationship is over. I want them to know that their mother and I value our relationship as parents and are still 100 percent devoted to working together to ensure our kids have the best of both of us.

It cannot be repeated enough: divorce is hard.

But it should not be any harder on the kids than it has to be, and it's up to the parents to make it as easy as possible.

If people truly love their kids and want the best for them, they will work on their post-divorce relationship with their former spouse. You must put aside your differences. You must work together to provide those kids with the same stable and drama-free upbringing they would have received in a two-parent home.

Your divorce is going to impact you greatly. It doesn't have to impact your kids greatly. Don't be a divorcé around your kids.

Just be their parent.

In 2023, I had the opportunity to serve alongside the legendary six-time Grammy Award winner Dionne Warwick as an executive producer for *Hits! The Musical*, a stage show that visited 48 cities across the United States.

Hits! The Musical was an unforgettable production of non-stop, foot-tapping fun and excitement for music lovers. It showcased 19 remarkable singers and 10 extraordinary dancers from all corners of the country. The budding young superstars took audiences on a musical journey, performing medleys of nearly 100 of America's most iconic songs, including classics such as "Hero," "Signed, Sealed, Delivered," "I Will Always Love You," and "Singing in the Rain."

In my opinion, a behind-the-scenes story is just as remarkable.

Another of the executive producers was Bob Gries, who has been a close friend of mine for many years and has supported me and the Bullard Family Foundation's work. His grandfather was a founding owner of the Cleveland Rams in 1936 and Cleveland Browns in 1946, and his family held a minority share in the football franchise until 1996, when Bob's father refused to be part of the franchise moving to Baltimore. Bob later owned Arena Football League teams in Tampa and Orlando.

The director of *Hits! The Musical* was Cynthia Nekvasil, the founder of Entertainment Revue, a song and dance ensemble that effectively served as a farm team for *American Idol* and who developed the all-female pop band P.Y.T., who toured with NSYNC and Britney Spears.

Bob and Cynthia are also a divorced couple. Yet they never stopped co-parenting and never stopped working together.

They met in 1993 when Entertainment Revue performed during halftime of the Hall of Fame Bowl in the old Tampa Stadium. Bob was there in attendance and was so impressed with the ensemble's talent that he asked them to perform at Tampa Bay Storm Arena Football League games.

One of the performers became a good luck charm of sorts. So when the Storm traveled to Detroit for the title game that year, she went along, and Cynthia went with her as a chaperone. The Storm won the championship and sparks flew between Bob and Cynthia, who had their first dinner date after the celebration.

Bob sold the Storm the following year to concentrate on financial investment. They married the next year and then adopted a daughter from China in 1999.

But they did not have a happily ever after. Actually, they did, but not as a married couple. They separated in 2008 and divorced in 2009. It was amicable, so much so that they used the same attorney. And they made a conscious decision to not let the differences that led to their divorce impact their child.

Bob admits that was easier than it would be in other divorces because their split wasn't caused by infidelity or any form of abuse. They just simply fell out of love. But they were mature enough to admit that they could still love one another as family.

Bob continued to run the Tampa Bay Volleyball Academy, which trained and sponsored 16 teams for girls aged 10 to 16, one of whom was their daughter. During games, Bob and Cynthia continued to sit together. They never displayed any hostility. They also spent holidays as a family, even after each remarried. Cynthia attended charity events sponsored by Bob, and Bob continued to attend shows put on by Cynthia.

Then in 2015, when Cynthia wanted to step away from Entertainment Revue to spend more time with their daughter, she struggled to find a worthy successor. Bob stepped up and volunteered to serve as short-term business advisor until they could be certain of its long-term future. The Revue is still around, with Bob serving as an advisor.

When asked how they never let their differences as a former married couple impact their parenting and business relationship, Bob said it was simple: you always put your kid first, and always remember that divorce doesn't mean you lose respect for your former spouse.

Bob and Cynthia are great people, great businesspeople, and great examples for all divorced couples.

———

I have won the WWE Tag Team Championship. I was the first ever 24/7 Champion. I was inducted into the WWE Hall of Fame as a recipient of the Warrior Award that honored my charity work.

I have plenty of highlights as a WWE Superstar, but it might shock you to learn of two on my list. They both include televised falls.

My first fall occurred while I was part of NXT, back when it was a competition with the winner receiving a WWE contract, rather than serving as its own promotion as it is today. One of the first contests was a race in which we had to carry a keg while running around the ring. Well, I tripped and fell and was the first contestant cut from the competition.

And the other, of course, is the most famous fall in WWE history, the trip known as the Titus World Slide: while racing to the match during *Greatest Royal Rumble* in Saudi Arabia, I slipped and slid under the ring.

Why are those highlights of my career?

Because they are proof of my mettle.

Either of those incidents could have ruined my career. I think they would have ruined many others' careers. But each time, I stood up, dusted myself off, and moved on.

We cannot let our mistakes own us. We must own the mistakes and then move on to greater things.

The same can be said for divorce. It's hard to move on to another relationship, to get back out there, and to put yourself on the line again. But you owe it to yourself to try.

And if you have children, you must remember that you are no longer just bringing a significant other into your life. You are bringing them into your family.

Yes, you can still date around. How else are you going to find the right one if you don't meet people? But you cannot get serious with someone until you are certain that they are serious about being a part of your family.

I have made a few mistakes. Any woman I date doesn't need to be my kids' mother. They have one—an excellent one. But a woman I date should want to support my kids. They should want to go to their games and birthday parties and celebrate all of their achievements. My kids are the most important part of my life, which means a woman who claims to love me should want to be a part of their life too. You cannot love me if you don't love my kids.

I have dated women who said and did all the right things early on. I have been fooled by women who pretended to be someone they are not, but their true self always came out. Ultimately, they could only fake my family's importance to them for so long.

I do have one post-divorce dating success story, though. Our romantic relationship did not succeed, but we remain close and, most importantly, her relationship with my sons did succeed and continues to thrive. If someone you are dating becomes important to your kids, they cannot simply ghost the children if the romantic relationship ends.

I met LaRhonda Jones in 2012. We started as friends and then became romantic. I was protective of my sons after a few bad relationships, so it took nearly a year before I was ready for them to meet LaRhonda. And she was okay with that and understood the wait. She never pressured me into introducing her to my children. That meant a lot.

I just did not want to waltz her through the door. I wanted the first time she met my sons to be special. So the two of us planned it out.

She would come over to my house, we would watch a movie as a foursome, and then I would introduce her as more than a friend, explaining that she was my new girlfriend, whom they would be seeing around quite often. We would then all go to an Arena Football League game to cheer on our hometown Tampa Bay Storm.

It could not have gone any better. We watched *Frozen*. I explained that LaRhonda was very special to me. And then she mentioned she was going to run home to change before we went to the game. Well, my sons did not want her to leave, so they ran upstairs to grab clothing options from their closets. She gushed with appreciation but told them she needed to wear her own clothes and would be back soon.

And like that, she was part of our lives. I stress "our," the three of us.

While some women want nothing to do with a man's kids, others try too hard to be a part of their life. LaRhonda played it perfectly. She never pressed. She came to their games and celebrations. She made a point to ask them about their days and offer advice in situations that would not step on my or their mother's toes. She told my sons she would always be there for them. Whatever they needed, she explained, they should never be afraid to ask. And over time, they warmed up and treated her like a member of our family. They called her their "bonus mom," and she called them her "bonus sons."

I would be lying if I said there wasn't an adjustment period for me too. They began going to her over me for advice in certain situations. "I'm their father," I thought, and I did not understand why they would go to her over me.

Then I remembered something we say in the WWE locker room: different people have different flavors. That is why WWE strives to have a diverse roster of unique personas. What works for one person might not work for another. So we try to offer something for everyone.

It's the same with raising children. There is a reason people say "it takes a village." The more options children have for advice and help, the better, and LaRhonda was a fantastic option for them to have in their lives.

I proposed to LaRhonda a year or so after I introduced her to my kids, and I made them a part of the proposal.

My sons had a flag football game that she, of course, was going to attend. She stopped by my house after work and then went upstairs to freshen up for the game. One of the boys called up to her, asking for help to find something. When she came downstairs, both my sons handed her a box with a ring and a note asking for her hand in marriage. I entered the room, she said yes, and we celebrated as a family.

But it did not work out—we never made it to the altar.

Four years after LaRhonda met my kids, we broke up. I told her that didn't mean she couldn't be part of my sons' lives, to which she sighed, smiled wide, and said, "I never want them out of my life."

I broke the news to my sons and then gave them alone time with LaRhonda. She assured them that even though she would not legally become their stepmother, she would remain their bonus mom. She wanted to keep talking with them on the phone, cheering them on at games, and going out for meals with them. And she lived up to her word. To this day, she remains a big part of their lives.

She is still important to me too. We successfully transitioned our romantic relationship back to a friendship.

She works with the Bullard Family Foundation and is still someone I know I can lean on during hard times.

I might go so far as to call her one of my best friends. But no, she is more than a friend. She is truly part of my family.

I know it might sound strange for someone to consider an ex-fiancée as part of their family, and it might be difficult for some women to handle, but in my opinion, if you are secure in who you are and what we are building together, LaRhonda would not be a threat because she is not that type of person. She would gracefully step out of the way and remain only a part of the kids' lives in a show of respect to the woman I have chosen to date or move forward with.

Some men might not want a former fiancée hanging around. It might seem awkward. They might toss the former fiancée to the curb if that friendship threatened another woman. I guess I'm not some men.

And if, in a hypothetical world, LaRhonda and I have a falling out so extreme that I want her out of my life . . . as long as my sons want her to be a part of their lives, she'll be a part of mine.

It's not about me. It's always about my kids first.

Yes, I'm a WWE Superstar and a WWE Global Ambassador. But I'm a dad first and foremost. Period.

CHAPTER 5

THE ROAD

I don't recall where I went or who I performed with during my first WWE road trip, but I will never forget that first trek to the Tampa International Airport to catch my flight.

In all my wisdom, I thought it would be a great idea to have the kids with me on the drive to the airport. I envisioned a Hallmark moment. I would get out of the car. They would open their doors and then jump into my arms for a strong goodbye hug.

Instead, Titus cried.

He cried that he did not want me to leave. He cried as I walked into the airport. And I was told he cried the entire way home.

He was too young to understand anything more than his daddy was leaving. He could not yet grasp that I would be back soon. Well, sooner than later.

Luckily, TJ understood and was able to calm his little brother.

I vowed to never take them to the airport for a sendoff again.

That was my first lesson as a traveling dad.

The Bullard men are 2-0 against the Manning men in football.

I was on the 1997 University of Florida squad that went into Tennessee and overcame a vintage 353-yard Peyton Manning throwing game to win 33-20.

And then 14 years later, my sons starred on the Berkeley Prep team that defeated Arch Manning's Newman High School team in New Orleans in a game broadcast on ESPN.com.

TJ tallied four solo and two assisted tackles in one heck of a defensive effort. As for Titus, he never suited up for the game. He tore his ACL during practice the day before.

At the time that he called me with the news, I was in Saudi Arabia, nearly 7,000 miles from where I wanted to be. His voice was in decent spirits, but I could tell how emotionally hurt he was. After all, he is my son and I know my kids.

The game was a big deal, nationally broadcast, against a quarterback who was considered the best in the nation and who was born into one of the most famous football families of all time. Plus, Titus was unsure how the injury would impact his play upon rehabilitation and return. He kept repeating that he had no idea how he injured himself. It happened during a routine play in a non-contact drill. All I could say was that it would be alright and that we would do everything in our power to get him healthy again. But, being so far from him, it was one of the few times I felt helpless and hopeless as a father. I was absolutely sick to my stomach.

I was already planning to be there for the Friday night lights game, but now I had to be there sooner.

So I called the WWE travel team and asked for earlier flights. They bumped up my intended flight to Chicago and then found me an earlier one to New Orleans. I met my son at the hotel, took him to the game and sat with him as he watched Berkley win 49-24. I then booked a flight for us to return home earlier than the team so we could get him to a doctor, ASAP.

WWE then allowed me to remain home with Titus until I felt he was ready for me to return to the road. While our tour of Saudi Arabia had come to an end at the time of his injury and I did not miss out on any action, I assure you that WWE would have let me return home early if Titus's injury had happened at the start of the tour. They would have rewritten all my segments to accommodate my family needs. Always keep in mind that this is a television show and that asterisk at the bottom of the tickets always says that cards are subject to change. The reality is, at any given moment, anything and everything can happen to the talent: sickness, injury, or family matters can keep someone from performing on any given day. And as always, if there is a case where I must go home early, there is no doubt in my mind that the show will go on and we will pick up where the previous episode left off.

Regardless of who the talent is, from Roman Reigns to Brock Lesnar to Becky Lynch to Bianca Belair, WWE, from top to bottom, is a big family, and they will make accommodations for any and all talent when needed.

I was largely left on my own as a kid growing up in South Florida. Most kids in my neighborhood were as well. Most of us shared a common trait: we were from a single parent home. Part of being in a single parent home meant that we had to figure out what we were going to eat, when we were going to eat, and how we were going to eat, because our parents had to work.

There is no question our parents did everything in their power to make sure we had the necessities. But, let's face it, we were poor. There were several occasions where some of us did not know when we were going to eat. If it hadn't been for our neighborhood's village mentality, some of us may not have eaten on any given day.

All the single parents had to work a lot to make ends meet in most cases, which meant they could not take vacation days, sick days, or unpaid days off to attend school functions or support us at a sporting or academic event. It also meant a lot of us went to school regardless of how we were feeling—with headaches, toothaches, and, in some cases, fevers.

But I will say this: under extreme circumstances, my mom would be there. My friends' parents would be there too. But keep in mind, I said "extreme." Otherwise, we were on our own.

In my adulthood and as I look at parenthood through a different lens, the extreme for me is much different than it was for my mother. The extreme for me means that I want to be at every function possible for my kids: holidays, birthdays, sporting events, school plays, first days of school, last days of school, the list goes on and on. I want to be there. And in most cases, I have fulfilled that desire to the best of my ability because I work for a company that understands family comes first.

The sports entertainment industry is far different today than it once was. The performers of yesteryear had the same stress as a single parent from my neighborhood, even if they were married and well off. It's something you often hear from stars of the past. They were paid only if they performed. That meant they had to be in that ring whether sick or injured, and no matter what was going on back home. Skipping a card or leg of a tour not only meant they did not get paid, but they also risked losing their spot to a performer who was willing to put career over everything. It was an unhealthy dynamic that hurt the performers and their families.

Things are totally different today, due to the McMahons.

Vincent and Linda McMahon started WWE as a family business and grew it into the multi billion-dollar enterprise that it is today without ever losing that family aspect.

On television storylines, the McMahons have been portrayed as the most dysfunctional family of all time. They've spewed vile words at one another, physically assaulted one another, and seemingly turned on one another on a weekly basis.

In real life, however, the McMahons are a loving family who understand what's important and that people come first.

They have unceremoniously helped countless talent, some of whom left the company on bad terms. They have helped talent get into rehab, whether for substance use or physical injuries. And they have never waved a big flag, screaming, "Look at how great we are!" They don't help people for the kudos. They do it because it's the right thing to do.

When my sons' Pop Warner football team made it to its first championship game, WWE let me leave the tour and found me a flight to see the game.

And when my brother passed away in June 2023, WWE helped me with grief counseling. Vince and Stephanie each personally called me to offer condolences and checked in on me regularly.

WWE's family-first attitude should be the policy in every company in this world.

In many cases, companies focus way too much on the bottom line and not nearly enough on what is truly important: the people. If an employee has a sick child or their kid's graduation or championship game, they should not fear losing their job for asking for the night off. Businesses cannot continue to hold their employees hostage from their families.

I understand there are exceptions, even for WWE. They cannot rewrite the main event of *WrestleMania* at the last moment so that the world champion can watch one of their children play little league. But for the most part, a company needs to be willing to bend when it can.

Parents need to know that putting their family first will not put them out of work.

This may sound cliché, but it's true: kids grow up fast and we all only have one life to live.

Parents should enjoy being parents because, sooner than you realize, kids become adults. No one should look back and regret that they did not spend enough time with their loved ones.

There are many perks and advantages that come with becoming a WWE Superstar, just as there are with becoming an NFL player, which was my original athletic goal.

But one staunch difference between WWE and the NFL is the level of celebrity. Yes, there are NFL players who are heavily marketed, but with WWE, each character is promoted globally. Also, while the NFL is seeking worldwide recognition, WWE is already an established global form of entertainment. You can name almost any continent, country, or city in the world, and I have either performed there multiple times or our shows have been broadcast there. It may seem unbelievable that I'm more recognizable than many players in the NFL, but consider the platform WWE provides its Superstars: we are enjoyed by fans in hundreds of countries and heard in more than 35 different languages. If you ask people from England or Japan to name five NFL Hall of Famers, most will be hard pressed to do so. But if you ask those same people to name five WWE Superstars, I bet they can do it.

In no way, shape, or form is this meant to take anything away from NFL players, who put their lives on the line on a consistent basis to play a great game. Like WWE Superstars, they make huge sacrifices with their bodies. I'm only speaking about the differences between our platforms, which is huge. The WWE's following is bigger than the NFL's, MLB's, NBA's and NHL's combined.

This added recognition has helped me in more ways than one, especially for what I can do for my community.

Thaddeus Bullard the defensive end could not do as much as Titus O'Neil the globally recognized WWE Superstar.

But the downside of being a WWE Superstar, for me, as a father, is the travel schedule.

In the NFL, you sleep in your bed four or five nights a week during away game weeks, and you are not on the road for a full year. There is an off-season in every sport, but there's no off-season in WWE, and although we are sports entertainment, *sport* comes first for a reason. It's hard on the body. On top of that, every week is like an away game for us. I would put my travel schedule up against that of any other professional sports league. Let another athlete walk in my wrestling boots for one year, and I guarantee that they would 100 percent agree that being in sports entertainment is tougher.

I'm on the road upwards of 270 to 280 days a year. We have over 300 events a year between television, premium live events, and non-televised shows. Plus, we have numerous community appearances, such as hospital visits and charity events, that all of us enjoy doing because most of us came from very humble beginnings. We know that having the opportunity to use our celebrity status for good is part of the blessing of the celebrity status.

Travel is easier today than it once was, if easier is the right word, considering it's still one heck of a travel schedule.

When I started with WWE, I would leave my house on a Friday and return on a Wednesday.

Then came the brand split.

When with *Raw*, I still leave on a Friday. I then have a non-televised event on Saturday, either another non-televised show or a premium live event on Sunday, live television on Monday, and then back home by Tuesday.

For *SmackDown*, I leave on a Thursday, do live television on Friday, a non-televised show on Saturday, either another non-televised show or a premium live event on Sunday, and then home.

If not for careful planning, my life could easily fall into total chaos.

Take packing, for instance.

I have been midway through a road trip and realized I forgot to pack enough suits or left my workout clothes on my bed. The workout clothes are easily remedied with a quick run to a store. But guys my size cannot just walk into a store and buy a suit off the rack. Well, I can, but that suit will be wearing me instead of me wearing the suit. It will be too big in some places and too small in others. And, yes, I can have someone FedEx me a suit from home, but I'm not the type of man who likes to spend money because I was forgetful, although I will if necessary.

You also don't want to carry too many suitcases. No matter the length of a trip, you don't want to drag three, four, or five suitcases through the snow or sand or even through an airport. It adds to your workload and is not practical.

Preferably, I always try to keep it to a two-suitcase limit, which is something else that is hard for a person my size. Big people wear bigger clothes.

Shoes are the most difficult item to pack. I have a size 17 foot and need to bring four pairs on a trip. I need my wrestling boots, workout sneakers, a nice pair of sneakers, and dress shoes.

Packing for a guy my size is like a game of *Tetris*.

Shoes go at the bottom, arranged so that they don't take up more than one layer. Then my clothes and then my toiletries and other such items.

Once in a city, I find out where I can get laundry done if the hotel doesn't have a service. I cannot pack my sweaty gym gear with my suit. No one wants to spend time with the guy in the smelly suit.

And even with all that planning, I might still find myself in clothing trouble. There have been trips where I have received a call the night before I expected to return home, telling me that the tour has been extended for a few days. One such time, I was sent to Alaska and wasn't packed for the cold weather. WWE helped us get the necessary clothing, but I then needed to figure out how to cram the new clothes into an already full suitcase.

Diet is another road-related issue.

Again, we are professional athletes, and we push our bodies to the limit on a daily basis, either while performing for WWE or training for our next performance. Without that off-season, we must treat our bodies like a temple 365 days a year, seven days a week, 24 hours a day.

I meal prep on occasion, but doing it means more bags to carry. But there are vegans in the industry, and finding a vegan option on the road is not always possible, so they must add meal prep to their long list of travel errands.

I try to map out restaurants in advance of a trip. Not only do I want each to be an example of that city's specialty cuisine, but it must be on my route. I cannot take a 90-minute detour just to visit a specific eatery.

The options don't have to be fine-dining experiences. Sometimes, it just means finding a fast-food restaurant that can best meet your craving and health needs. Grilled chicken at a fast-food restaurant might not be as good as it would be at a five-star restaurant, but it's still grilled chicken.

Then there is my exercise routine.

I work out five days a week, waking at 4:30 every morning to do so.

To make sure I have options when on the road, I belong to several gym chains, and I sometimes call friends who work at the local college for permission to use their facilities.

Back home, outside of health and wellness, I also have the Bullard Family Foundation that runs my charity events, and I have investments in businesses throughout the Tampa Bay area and beyond. To help with those, I have a team of people who work for me, plus an attorney and a brand manager.

Everything I do in life takes planning.

And that includes being a dad.

And so I insist on finding time for that.

Since I have just about always been home on a limited basis due to my travel schedule, first as a football player and then as a WWE Superstar, I have always made sure to schedule time with my kids, even on my busiest days. Whenever I'm home, I make note of the dates, times, and places of every athletic practice and game or whatever other activity is important to them.

Being a dad is a privilege. It's about family and love. But it's also a job. It's the best job there is, but a job nonetheless. And, like any job, it takes scheduling and dedication.

That is not to say I have never missed anything and always been there for them.

Sure, I have had to miss out on some things.

There have been school events, first dates, and big games on the football field and basketball court that I only know about through their stories and videos.

But I have done everything I could to limit missing important moments. I have missed only a few birthdays and have always made up for that right before or shortly after the special day.

I have never missed a major holiday and I have always flown my children to be with me on Father's Day.

But most importantly, when I'm home, I'm home.

I don't need to call out names, but if you are a longtime fan of sports entertainment, I'm sure you have heard of countless examples of men from my industry who say they were on the road so often they were never comfortable at home. They would plop their suitcase on the living room floor, sit on the couch, and immediately started counting the minutes until they were back on the road. The industry became their life.

There are people like that in every profession, whether they travel or not. For some people, work becomes their life. And then they grow older. They have a Ferrari and a 10,000-square-foot home that make people jealous, but they are the ones who are jealous of the close bond that others have with their children. They never took a step back from work or the grind. They became what they did for a living.

I have always sought to be the opposite.

Being on the road is part of my job. Once I'm off the road, I'm no longer working. I will not miss my children's games so that I can sit down and watch tapes of my matches, nor will I cut my kids off mid-sentence so I can take a work call, unless it's 110 percent necessary. When I'm with my children, I'm a father first and foremost—period.

Some might fear that such an approach will hurt their career. But, if anything, the balance my family provides me has enhanced my career. You cannot spend 100 percent of your time doing one thing and not see voids in your life. A person who works out 24/7 and doesn't take the time for leisure activities will eventually get hurt. Those who focus on their career alone will eventually wake up and realize that their most important relationships have suffered.

We all want to be there for those key firsts in our children's lives: first step, first word, first day of school, first game, first date, and so on. But what many seem to forget is that some of the best moments with our children are those we cannot foresee. It may be a conversation while on a random walk to the park, a joke we share while watching a movie on the couch, a funny incident we witness while out to lunch, a key piece of advice we provide late at night, and so on.

Those moments are unplanned, but they cannot happen unless we plan time for our kids.

Life should never become so busy that you don't have time for your kids every day, even if that means a phone call while on the road or during a long day of meetings or a few text messages reminding your children you love them and believe in them.

We all must take a moment to make a moment.

For me, personally, fatherhood has always been my ultimate goal. Through divorce, through ups and downs, through life's trials and tribulations, my primary concern has always been to be a great man and a great father to my children. I don't apologize about this approach; for me, it's the most popular decision I can make.

I firmly believe that if it wasn't for my relationship with my children, my success would be meaningless and I would not have reached this level of success.

I have always sought to live my life in a way that makes my sons proud, and that means never submitting to any temptations, substance use or otherwise. That decision is what has enabled me to make such a difference in this world. While there are many people who have been far more successful than me in a WWE ring or football field, outside of those two places they have left far less of a mark on the world than I have.

Although I have great memories of the places I visited and the matches and titles on the road, some of my greatest moments while traveling were receiving texts from people saying they had met my children that day and all three were impressive young adults, and calls from my children saying they miss me and wished they could hug me or that they are proud of me.

My mother taught me a lot about being a great human being. My dad taught me a lot about what a man should be.

The Boys Ranch taught me a lot about how applying myself, respecting others, and believing in myself could yield success.

My children taught me the greatest lesson, one that I'm still learning on a consistent basis: how to be a better man.

Sure, my dad gave me advice and showed me the way, but my sons gave me firsthand experience and on-the-job training of what it takes to become a more responsible man. They taught me that being responsible and showing compassion could help to make me a great man. If I had not always been present in my children's lives, I would be a different person today.

It takes a lot of work to be a parent, but one thing is head and shoulders above everything else: be present. Even if you cannot be present all the time, be present during every moment that you can. We all have a long list of priorities. If you can find time for anything else on that list, you have to find time to be a father first because that should be your top priority.

———

Mr. Blalock is my dad, but I had another father figure in my life.

I also refer to Pastor Gregory Powe Sr. as a dad. He became my spiritual dad.

Pastor Powe, like Mr. Blalock, changed my life forever. He not only challenged me to be the best father I could be, but also the best man I could be. By being so, God, he said, would be able to use me in greater ways.

Pastor Powe would say my profession had nothing to do with why or how God used me. It did not matter if I played football or was a WWE Superstar. It was truly about what God saw in me as a man and in my heart.

When you talk about another rebellious spirit, you can look no further than Pastor Greg Powe Sr. While many people did not understand me and my wild ideas, he did because he too had wild ideas.

He unfortunately unexpectedly died in March 2017 at the tender young age of 62, but not before making a profound impact on my spiritual growth and a significant impact on the lives of thousands around the globe.

The annual Joy Giving holiday event was born at Revealing Truth Ministries. It grew from being held at our church, providing around 200 families with gifts and toys, into one of the largest holiday events in the Tampa Bay area, serving food, meals, clothing, toys, and gifts to more than 37,000 families per year during the Thanksgiving and Christmas seasons.

When, years ago, I spoke with Pastor Powe about moving the event from the church into the community, he was 100 percent in support of doing so because of my reasoning. It was simple. We both wanted to reach more people, and we knew that those we wanted to serve may or may not have the same religious beliefs. We wanted people from all walks of life to feel welcomed, those who wanted to give and those who were ready to receive. And we wanted both to do so with joy in their hearts and on their faces.

The event did well while at the church, but it turned into a greater movement outside of it. It went from the church to nice parks to Raymond James Stadium through collaborative partnerships with various organizations and partners through my Bullard Family Foundation. We have been able to put smiles on people's faces and hope in people's hearts.

If Pastor Powe had not given me the freedom and the wherewithal to allow God to use me as He intended, I don't know that this would have been possible. It took two outrageous rebellious thinkers doing what God has called us to do to turn a wild idea into a transformational reality.

I could go on and on about the ways Pastor Powe impacted my life and conversations that we had on various topics. But his largest impact was simply reminding me that it's okay to fail, and it's okay to be imperfect, as long as we recognize those faults and imperfections and seek to improve ourselves. People cannot hold you hostage to your faults when you already know what they are. They cannot demean you or embarrass you if you have accepted your faults and readily continue to work on them. All men and women have their faults and their imperfections. Nobody is perfect.

During my early days attending the services he led, he proclaimed, "God is going to elevate you, but he can't elevate you until you get out of your own way." I did not understand what he meant but wanted to know more since I was going through my own personal struggles as well as struggling in my marriage. When the service was done, I stuck around to talk.

He let me know those were not just words he preached. They were a way of life that he was living.

Pastor Powe was in long-term recovery from alcohol use disorder. It had been decades since his last sip of alcohol, but, as all afflicted with that disease, he was always in recovery, both as an individual and a family man.

His son, Bryan, who now runs Revealing Truth Ministries, said his earliest memories of his father can best be summed up as an "in and out dad." He could not hold down a job, so the bulk of the financial burden fell to his wife. And he was never fully present as a father, physically or in spirit. He missed athletic and school events. When home, he did not pay full attention to his children.

Then one day, when Bryan was around six or seven years old, Pastor Powe stopped drinking. Just like that, with no help. He did not attend a rehab clinic or have a counselor or support group. He just looked in the mirror one day, did not like the man looking back, and made a promise to God to live a more virtuous life. I'm not saying that all people should go that route or that seeking help from professionals is the wrong way to go. Most, nearly all people, need professional help. But, for whatever reason, Pastor Powe did not. Actually, I do know the reason: God.

He became an assistant pastor at a church in Atlanta. It was through the church that Pastor Powe learned to live and learned to love both himself and others. For him, the Bible was less about religion and more about instructions for living and loving. And he wanted to take his experiences and what he learned from God and share it with others. He wanted to let others know that being a sinner doesn't mean they must die a sinner. He wanted people to know that even if their beginning wasn't very good, their ending could still be special.

In 1990, Pastor Powe, his wife, Deborah, and four children, Gregory, Christopher, Bryan, and Chrystle, came to Tampa from Atlanta. Pastor Powe and his wife then founded the ministry that grew to three Florida campuses and thousands of parishioners who believed in their message because they knew it was real and from the heart.

In 1998, Pastor Powe then started the Greg Powe Ministries as an outreach of Revealing Truth Ministries to share his message with the world. He crisscrossed the globe, from India to Ukraine to the Caribbean to South America to Africa.

He transformed from a man in search of a purpose to a man making an international difference.

And he made a difference at home too.

The once "in and out dad" became an all-in dad. Because of travels and God's mission for him, Pastor Powe, like me, could not always be at everything for his kids, but he was at most sporting events, school activities, parent-teacher meetings, and the like. He never missed a major holiday. He never missed a birthday. He took his children on business trips and regular vacations. He created memories, and he lived in the moment whenever he was with his family.

Bryan has a favorite memory of his father. But it has nothing to do with an elaborate trip, expensive gift, or grand gesture.

One afternoon, Bryan had a roller hockey game. When he looked into the stands, he saw his father wearing a three-piece suit. Pastor Powe stood out among the other parents wearing jeans and T-shirts. The other parents had time to go home to change after work. Pastor Powe did not. He had to be uncomfortable. It was hot in that gym, Bryan said, and his father knew it would be. But he rushed right over so as not to miss a moment of the game.

Teammates lovingly clowned Bryan because his father was dressed so dapper at such an event. But Bryan wasn't embarrassed at all. To him, that three-piece suit was a symbol of his father's love.

That's Bryan's favorite memory. Pastor Powe had given him the greatest gift: time.

I was heartbroken when my spiritual father passed away. Selfishly, I wanted more time with him. I felt that he had more advice to give me, but I now know that God was ready for him because Pastor Powe had fulfilled his mission here on Earth. He taught the people of this world how to become better and reminded them that it's never too late to do so.

If you are reading this and realize that you could be more present with your children, go make that change.

Find a moment to make a moment.

CHAPTER 6

ADOPTION
AND MENTORING

I very easily could not have been born.

When my grandmother learned about the circumstances of her daughter's pregnancy, she ordered her to have an abortion. Regardless of what transpired back then, my grandmother will always be one of my favorite people. When my mother refused to terminate her pregnancy, my grandmother threw her out of the house. My mother gave birth to me as a scared 12-year-old child. She made a brave choice.

Some people who know my situation have tried to use me as an example in the pro-life/pro-choice debate. I have never, nor will I ever, pick a side.

Still, I'm unabashedly pro adoption.

If you find yourself in a situation where your concern is raising the baby, remember, there are a lot of people out there who would bring your child into their home and call the baby their own.

If you have the means to adopt and the time to raise a child, you should. Open your home and life up to a child in need of a family.

If you don't have the means to raise a child full-time but can mentor a child in need of guidance, you absolutely should do so. And in some cases, you *must* do so.

Blood alone doesn't make a parent or parental figure.

While my mother's brave decision gave me life, mentors are the ones who gave me *this* life.

There was Coach Bump.

My childhood Pop Warner football coach, Mathew "Bump" Mitchell, was a Black police officer who worried more about turning us into fine young men than winning football games. Oh, we won a lot of football games. We were dominant, but it was Coach's off-the-field lessons that stick with me the most.

Coach Bump was very much like Tony Dungy. He kept a level head and preferred to talk to us like young men rather than to scream and hoot and holler.

But Coach Bump most impacted me with his actions.

He was known for having a soft spot for troubled young men. He would more often put a young man in the back of his police car for a stern lecture or caring talk rather than for a drive to the station. He knew the solution wasn't incarceration. Rather, the solution was rehabilitation.

When I was suspended from school on one occasion, Coach Bump was worried I would get into trouble when left home alone, since my mother had to work, so he took me to work with him. He left me alone in a room at the station, gave me busy work, and popped in every few hours to remind me that actions have consequences that I needed to be better behaved, and that I could make a big difference in the world, but not from jail.

And then there was Patrick Monogue, the head of the Florida Sheriffs Boys Ranch.

Early in my time there, he noticed I was keeping ranch employees at arm's distance. I refused to become part of the ranch family.

He sought me out, and we bonded over games of pickup basketball. Knowing I was in need of a mentor, he filled that role for me on campus.

He stood up for me when much of his staff wanted me thrown out. I was still a young man filled with anger. They wrongly worried I would turn violent and hurt someone, maybe even one of them.

But Mr. Monogue knew I would not attack an adult, and he was more worried about what would become of me if I left the ranch. So he sat me down and said the words that changed my life.

When he asked why I was always getting into trouble, I answered, "I don't know. I'm just a bad kid." He replied, "There is no such thing as a bad kid," which has since become my mantra.

He then said, "I love you and I believe in you," which instantly changed my life. He was the first person to ever tell me he believed in me. It meant the world to me. I wanted to prove that I deserved that compliment and sought to turn my life around. That is all it took.

Mr. Monogue told me to come to him whenever I needed someone. I took him up on that offer again and again until his death in 1997.

Coach Bump, Mr. Monogue, and my dad, Mr. Blalock, each represent a different level of mentorship that you can mimic.

Coach Bump mentored me as part of a larger group of young men who played football for him. He would then help players on an individual basis when needed.

Mr. Monogue took specific one-on-one interest in me.

And though Mr. Blalock never legally adopted me, he became my dad.

I owe each of those men and others my eternal gratitude.

Now I seek to pay it forward, and I'm not alone in doing so. Countless others serve as mentors. Join us, in whatever capacity you can.

As I mentioned, it takes a village to raise a child. Take initiative. Join the village. I can promise you that it will be one of the most gratifying decisions you will ever make in your entire life.

———

For years, my friend Ricky Sailor's only memory of his mother was of the Burger King at which she worked. He recalled sitting at a table at the fast-food restaurant and playing with a kid's-meal figurine of a ThunderCat, a popular science fiction cartoon from our youth. And he remembered his mother regularly bringing home a single burger to be split between him, his two brothers, and two sisters.

That was it. That was all he knew about his mother.

She left when he was four years old, which divided the family. Ricky's older brother and sister had a different father, so they had to go live with him. Ricky and his little brother stayed with their dad.

For much of his childhood, Ricky swore to himself that a woman in his neighborhood was his mother. He never voiced that belief to friends but internalized it to the point that he 100 percent believed it was true.

She wasn't his mother. But he did get a brief opportunity to meet his biological mom.

Ricky forged a relationship with his maternal great-grandmother. So when she passed away during his freshman year of college, he planned to return home to Tampa to attend her funeral. But someone else would be there too, his older brother said. Their biological mother.

He planned to meet her at his great-grandmother's house, where the family was gathering. He knocked and then greeted the woman who answered as his mother.

"No, baby, I'm not your mother," the woman said. "She is in the back."

Ricky walked to the living room at the back of the house. His mother was sitting there with three other kids. She introduced herself and the children, who were Ricky's other siblings.

"Hold on," Ricky thought, "you raised them but did not want to raise me?"

He swallowed his hurt. He wanted a mother.

Ricky's college roommate spoke to his mother on the phone once a week, so that is what he envisioned a relationship to be like. He asked if they could talk once a week. His biological mother said yes.

She never called.

A year later, he found a real mother.

Throughout high school, from afar, Ricky looked up to his friend's mother, Sheila Allen, whom he met through a community organization that worked with children.

To Ricky, she represented everything he wanted in a mom. She was typically there for her daughter's events and often picked her up from school. She bragged about her children to anyone who would listen, and Ricky would often hear his friend mention that her mother was her best friend and someone in whom she could confide.

Knowing Ricky was without a mom, Sheila took extra interest in him.

Nothing major; she asked how his day was, congratulated him on athletic achievements, and told him to cheer up when she noticed he was down. She would have praised his good grades but, well, Ricky needed to get good grades first.

To Ricky, she began to feel like a mother. During his sophomore year of college, he decided to make it official.

Sheila was a travel agent who put together and led day trips to other cities, sometimes inviting Ricky to tag along.

On the way home from one such trip to Miami, Sheila was sitting one seat in front of Ricky. He decided to move to the seat next to her and lay his head in her lap. As she stroked his head, he knew that was what he wanted. It felt right. It felt motherly.

He built up the courage over the next few weeks, and one day, just as I did with Mr. Blalock, he asked if she would be his mother.

She sweetly said, "Yes, baby. I will be your mother."

And from that moment on, she was.

They spoke more than once a week on the phone. She would visit him at college and cheer him on when he played football. She bragged about Ricky to friends and told him how proud she was of everything he did. Most importantly, she was always there for him when needed.

She is Ricky's mom to the point that he writes *Sheila Allen* on documents asking for his mother's name.

But besides a mother, Ricky also found a strong male mentor.

If you are a football enthusiast whose fandom dates to the 1970s and 1980s, you might know the name Tyrone Keys.

As a defensive end, he recorded 26 sacks for Mississippi State, where he was selected to three consecutive All-Southeastern Conference teams and, during his senior season, helped the team break Alabama's 25-game winning streak and earn a berth in the 1980 Sun Bowl.

He was drafted by the New York Jets but chose to play with the British Columbia Lions in the Canadian Football League for two seasons before joining the NFL as a member of the Chicago Bears and their vaunted 1986 Super Bowl–winning defense. During the Bears' famed "Super Bowl Shuffle" music video, Mr. Keys can be seen playing the keyboard.

Like most people I look up to, Keys's off-field contributions top anything he did on the gridiron.

Once Mr. Keys retired from football, he moved to Tampa full-time and worked as a counselor and advisor at Tampa Catholic, while also assisting young men and women throughout the area.

In 1993, Albert Perry from Leto High School was among those who sought out Mr. Keys, who then helped the young football star put together highlight films and study for college admission tests.

Albert earned a scholarship to Texas Southern, but he never went.

Mr. Keys bumped into the young man in Tampa a few weeks after he was supposed to have reported to campus. Albert told

Mr. Keys he didn't have a way to get there, and then Albert said, "If I don't get out of here, I'll end up dead or in trouble."

A week later, Albert was shot to death.

Mr. Keys became determined to do more for young men and women.

The same year Albert was killed, Mr. Keys founded All Sports Community Services, which provides scholarships to at-risk youth throughout the nation while mentoring them through a combination of academic support, required community service, and athletics. The nonprofit has provided tens of millions of dollars in scholarships and shaped countless young men and women into leaders.

My friend Ricky is one of them.

His dad was a great father. But he also worked long days of very hard back-breaking labor. He left the house at 6 a.m. each weekday and returned at 6 p.m. completely wiped out. He was attentive on weekends, but not as much as he would have liked. He sometimes needed to rest his aching body.

Ricky starred for Leto High School as a cornerback but was admittedly getting into the type of minor trouble that could have turned major.

So when Mr. Keys was tipped off about Ricky not fulfilling his potential, he approached him in Leto's hallway and did not mince words, much as Mr. Blalock did to me. He was there to help Ricky get into college and make something of himself. If he wanted that to happen, this was his chance, Mr. Keys said. If he did not, then it was so long. Ricky said yes.

Just as he did for Albert, Mr. Keys made sure Ricky took school more seriously and learned how to navigate the recruiting process. But through his nonprofit, Mr. Keys was able to go beyond what he did for Albert.

Mr. Keys made sure Ricky did not have idle time for trouble. When Ricky wasn't in school or on the football field, he was with Mr. Keys, performing community service. Sometimes, Ricky just joined Mr. Keys as he ran errands. All along, Ricky watched Mr. Keys, soaked in all that he did, and sought to mimic him. Eventually, Mr. Keys celebrated Ricky's turnaround with a gift: a football jersey with the No. 23, which was Albert's number.

Ricky went on to star for Butte College and then Texas Tech, with Mr. Keys always watching over Ricky's shoulder. One time, when Ricky mentioned to Mr. Keys that he had not had Fruity Pebbles in a while, a care package with a box of cereal was sitting at Ricky's front door just three days later. It wasn't so much the cereal that Ricky was happy to see—although I'm certain he enjoyed it—it was just knowing that Mr. Keys had listened to him.

And Ricky later paid it forward by founding Unsigned Preps, an organization designed to assist high school student athletes obtain admission into college. Built on positioning exposure, education, community service, and consulting as the keys to effectively producing well-rounded student athletes that flourish on college campuses, they have mentored countless youth by mimicking Mr. Key's foundation.

Ricky was raised by a village and then joined a village. He is proof that blood is not needed to be someone's parent or parental figure.

Alle was convinced that Titus was going to be a girl.

She told me she was pregnant over dinner at a restaurant in Fort Myers. She ordered dessert, a slice of cake, and inside was a little note that said "Surprise, we're pregnant." The note was written on pink stationery, symbolizing that the baby was going to be a girl, even if it was way too soon to know.

At the time, I was on the fence about whether I wanted a girl.

I was more than prepared to be a father of two but was unsure if I was ready for barrettes and doing hair and the whole daddy's little girl/"Girl Dad" thing. But Alle was so convinced the baby would be a girl, we even debated names for her. I liked Ruby and Tatyana.

Of course, Tatyana turned out to be Titus, my WWE Superstar namesake. It seemed fitting. I named my first son after me, and my WWE persona after my second son.

I breathed a sigh of relief when the doctor told us that the baby was a boy, but I still wanted a girl someday, when I was ready. I began to consider adoption when I had hit a point in my life and career where days and nights were too hectic to properly raise a third baby.

I almost adopted two seven-year-old sisters in 2015.

As Hurricane Irma barreled down on Florida, I sent my sons to Louisiana for safety but stayed behind to help the Florida Sheriffs Youth Ranch's kids through the ordeal. While sheltering there and trying to remain a positive voice during a scary time, I fell in love with two sisters who had been part of the foster care system prior to being taken in by the ranch.

I knew I had the means and ability to add the girls to my family, so I began to go through the adoption process before learning that their parents had changed their minds.

I was hurt. I had my heart set on becoming a Girl Dad.

Little did I know I already knew the young lady who would help me fill that role.

The Academy Prep Center of Tampa is one of the places where I mentor.

The middle school is located in the Ybor/East Tampa area and is specifically for disadvantaged students who are considered at-risk because, for instance, they live in a dangerous neighborhood with one parent who must work long hours. So, through need-based scholarships and donor support that provide free tuition, children are at the school 11 hours a day, six days a week, so that they have a safe and nurturing environment.

I regularly visit the school to speak with the children, both as part of a class and one-on-one.

I also help with fundraisers.

In 2013, I hosted a fashion show at the school and brought with me fellow WWE Superstars Darren Young, Sheamus, Wade Barrett, Drew McIntyre, Justin Gabriel, Jimmy Uso, Cesaro, Damien Sandow, AJ Lee, Vickie Guerrero, Natalya, Aksana, Naomi, Summer Rae, Paige, and Alicia Fox.

The fashion show featured clothing inspired by the 1930s and '40s, with casual, semi-formal, and formal wear created by a few designers, including those who worked for WWE.

Money was raised through ticket sales and a silent auction.

That is how I met Kerry McDonald.

She was there in support of her friend whose business had donated to the auction. Sandra Gray, one of the WWE's fashion designers at the time, then roped Kerry into modeling for the event. Kerry, a shy woman, was mortified and traumatized by the experience, but it's also why I noticed her.

Following the show, I thanked her for the help, and over small talk, we became friends.

Then as the years ticked by, we saw more and more of one another because of our kids. Her daughter, Leah, and my sons all played AAU basketball. Though she competed in the girls tournaments and TJ and Titus were in the boys bracket, we would often grab lunch or dinner during those long weekends of games and cheer on one another's children.

In time, I became attached to Leah, loved her, and sought to fill a fatherly role for her.

Her biological father wasn't married to her mother and left them six or seven months after Leah was born. He came back into their lives for a short time in 2015, but no real fatherly relationship was established.

Kerry is a tremendous single mother, but Leah wanted a father too.

On Father's Day each year, Kerry sought to distract her daughter by planning fun activities for the two of them, but Leah would at times ask why she did not have a dad. Kerry would typically say that sometimes relationships don't work out and that some men are not cut out to be fathers. She was always diplomatic. She never wanted to speak down about Leah's biological father in case he came back into her life.

For Kerry, the hardest part of being a single mother was simply time, or lack thereof. She was a nurse who needed to work long hours to provide for Leah, but she had little support. She was born in Canada, had no family here, and was hesitant to bring a boyfriend into Leah's life because she did not want to risk her daughter losing yet another father figure if the relationship did not work out.

That is where I stepped in.

My relationship with Kerry has never been anything but platonic. That meant I wasn't going anywhere, and I knew I would never abandon Leah.

My early role was simple: I just wanted to be her male role model. If she asked for advice, I offered my opinion but did not press. Our relationship then continued to grow, and she spent so much time with my sons that they became more like siblings than friends.

I often lamented to Kerry that I had always wanted a daughter and that I was always open to making Leah a part of my family through adoption. It would not change much logistically, I explained. Kerry and I would remain friends and live in separate homes, but Leah would legally be my daughter in case anything ever happened.

Then something did happen.

Without getting into specifics, Kerry had a health scare.

It became a concern that Leah would have to move to Canada to live with family if something ever happened to Kerry. Besides the trauma of losing her mother, she would then be uprooted from everything she knew: her hometown, school, sports teams, friends.

In 2022, I decided to again ask about adoption, but really push for it this time.

I first asked my sons if they would be okay with it. And just as Mr. Blalock's three children accepted me as a sibling almost immediately, my sons gave me the thumbs-up. Their only concern was whether or not Leah could handle our competitiveness. I reminded them of all the times we played basketball together and how she never backed down or played the role of damsel in distress when things got rough. She was willing to get as physical as it took to win.

I texted Kerry that I would adopt Leah to protect her if the worst-case scenario ever occurred, and that TJ and Titus were on board with it too. Radio silence followed for about 20 minutes. I worried that meant the answer was no and that I had overstepped my boundaries.

Then my phone rang. It was Leah. She was crying, and the 20-minute delay was so she could collect herself.

"Why are you doing this for me?" she asked.

"Actually, I'm not just doing it for you," I replied. "I'm doing it for me too. I have always wanted a daughter just like you, and my sons have always wanted a sister just like you. I'm adopting you because I love you and because I think you are a great human being. Just as Mr. Blalock came along and became that father figure to me, I want to be that for you. I promise that if you say yes, I'm not going to try to overly father you and change you. I just want to help you become the best version of you who can do amazing things in school and both on and off the basketball court."

She said yes. *She said yes!*

And, like that, I had a 16-year-old daughter.

At that moment, I was as happy as when both my sons were born. Maybe happier since this experience did not involve needles.

That night, I attended Leah's basketball game. And, of course, she dominated.

After the game, Kerry suggested that Leah and I talk in person.

I don't recollect the conversation, but I will never forget her face. She kept smiling and laughing. She was so happy. I was the same. We had both been given a great gift.

Kerry would later tell me that on the way home Leah said something along the lines of "I cannot believe he wants to be my dad."

She deserves a dad who loves her.

I thank God on a near daily basis that the worst has not happened and appears it never will. Kerry's health has been fine.

A year after Leah said yes, we made it legally official. And my relationship with Leah has flourished as a father-daughter relationship. I go to as many of her basketball games as I can. We talk daily, text throughout the day, and spend one-on-one time together throughout the week.

Kerry likes to joke that she feels like the odd one out at times because I have somehow taken on the role of the cooler parent. I cannot help that. I'm cool. What can I say?

Kerry has been great, though.

She doesn't treat me like a "sort of" father. Rather, we often talk as co-parents, whether it's about a big decision like college or something small like a hairstyle.

Well, to be honest, the hairstyle thing seemed like a big deal.

Leah wanted to buzz some of her hair on the side of her head but was worried her mother would be against that style because it wasn't girly enough.

So Leah called me and relayed her fear.

I then called Kerry, who wasn't just fine with the haircut but was also thrilled that Leah called me. It showed that she had another sounding board for advice and support.

I will forever be there for Leah, just as I will always be there for TJ and Titus, and just as Mr. Blalock is always there for me.

But Mr. Blalock and I are not unique.

There are plenty of others who have done the same for children, and I hope there are plenty more who will continue to do the same.

CHAPTER 7

HOW TO SPOIL CHILDREN (WITHOUT RAISING SPOILED CHILDREN)

You have surely heard the cliché that money cannot buy health and happiness.

I would tend to agree that is true to a certain point in life. Life can be very crazy and challenging at times, and there will always be certain things that money, celebrity, and status cannot buy. Yes, having access to money and resources can get you better food, better physical trainers, better mental health, and better medical access. And yes, this is a very sad truth about our society that many don't want to admit. After living on both sides of the equation, I can honestly say that this is very close to the truth, closer to the truth than a lie.

It's well documented that I am someone who grew up with much of nothing. Financial and other barriers inhibited not only me but also others in my environment from achieving health and prosperity.

So many people have asked me how I make so much time to help others. My immediate response is how can I not make time when so many people, many of whom were strangers and still are strangers, made time for me? There were so many people who helped put me in the position that I'm in today, and equally as important, there are several people who help me continue down this path that I'm on.

There is no question that I have a lot of great things at my fingertips. I can travel to where I want to. I can go to any event I want to go to. And I can do it the way I want to do it without any restraints.

The most rewarding part of this is that I get to do this with my children and for my children. I cannot make this world a better place without first and foremost uplifting and providing for my own children.

Some people might say I spoil my kids. Maybe.

Some people might say my children are spoiled. Absolutely not. Those people, if they had a single conversation with my children, would realize that they are 100 percent wrong.

Some people wrongly associate living a privileged life with being spoiled. But you can shower your children with gifts, yet raise them to appreciate what they have, to not expect more than what you are willing to give, and to still want to make their own way in life. You can raise kids in a very privileged environment and still teach them to be great human beings; to respect people; to understand that, as blessed as we are, there are people who are not as fortunate and that it's our obligation to help lift people up. Sometimes, all it takes is just being kind to another person and being empathetic and sympathetic to others' situations.

My children have certainly lived privileged lives and have access to more than most.

As I alluded to earlier, money cannot buy health. But it certainly helps.

A few years back during TJ's senior football season, he was having issues with his back to the point that he had to miss a couple of games. He had already committed to play for the University of Central Florida, so the issue wasn't going to impact his future. But my son was and is a competitor, as everyone in my family is, and it was going to impact his present. More importantly, it was going to impact his team as they fought to earn their ticket to the state playoffs and hopefully a state championship.

He wanted to play. As his father, I was going to do whatever I could to ensure he was healthy enough to do so.

We took him for a CAT scan and then scheduled a follow-up appointment to hear the results. The appointment was for Wednesday, days before the next big game under the Friday night lights, but the medical facility canceled it five minutes before we got there. So we booked another appointment for Thursday. It too was canceled at the last moment. We were angry and frustrated, but it turned out there was nothing nefarious or bumbling about the cancelation. The specialist we were supposed to see had come down with COVID.

Friday morning rolled around. TJ's game time was hours away. We were still in the dark. He felt much better and was limber and strong enough that I felt safe letting him put on the pads and helmet. But my gut feeling and his gut feeling alone were not going to allow me to let him step out on that field. I wasn't going to send him out to get hit or to hit anyone without a doctor's permission. As a dad, my primary job is to protect my children, sometimes from themselves until they are old enough to make those decisions on their own. TJ wanted to play and would have gone out there without an okay from a medical professional. Heck, he would have gone out there without pads or a helmet.

TJ's mother took him to the doctor that Friday morning. They were finally able to see him, sort of. A doctor wasn't available, but a nurse was. Her first question was "How long have you been battling cancer?" There was a spot on his back that looked cancerous, apparently. The nurse thought that someone had already broken the news to him.

Alle's heart dropped. She called me and put me on speaker to talk with the nurse. My heart dropped too. It was my son's senior year. He was at the top of the mountain. His future looked brighter than the sun on a hot Florida summer day. But just like that, everything could be snatched away from him. Everything.

We wanted more information, but the nurse could not provide anything else. We needed to speak with a doctor, she said, but none were available. Look, I'm a reasonable and thoughtful guy. Most of the time. But at that moment, it took all the restraint I could muster to keep a level head. At that moment, losing my temper would not have accomplished anything. Asking more questions to a nurse who seemingly had no answers would have accomplished nothing more than increased frustration. So I did what I would do on any other occasion when my family is under attack. I went into prayer. I spoke against any hurt, harm, or danger to any of my family members. And I declared that my son was free of cancer, refuting the medical possibility.

This was also a time for me to utilize the access that I gained over years from helping countless others, not only throughout the Tampa Bay area but the world. It's well documented that I have used my platform, whether it be as an athlete, football player, or WWE Superstar, to help thousands of others. So I have sown a lot of good into the world, and I have gained a lot of access to resources and developed long-standing relationships with people.

So aside from praying and speaking and refuting against the poor prognosis, I also began to act, first by calling the medical facility's CEO, with whom I have a close relationship, to tell him how my son's and my family's experience was horrible.

The doctor called me within 10 minutes. But even that doctor was kind of smug, lecturing that we seemed more worried about my son playing football than his health. Again, I took a deep breath.

No, I explained, our concern is his health, but we don't know anything about his health. Not a single doctor has yet to see him. A nurse told us that it might be cancer and we are scared, worried, and annoyed that we are in the dark because several doctor's appointments were canceled out of the blue. And now, hopefully, you can understand why there's angst.

He then continued to go back and forth with me until I finally told him what I thought of him in the strictest of terms—well, I defined him with one word that describes the piece of the body attached to our thighs. I very rarely go off on anyone, but I was over it.

I hung up the phone and immediately called the CEO of another medical facility. We got TJ an immediate appointment. I picked up his results from the previous facility, dropped them off at the new one, and scheduled a virtual appointment for my son.

The doctor did not mince words. He could not rule out cancer 100 percent. But he also said he wouldn't know for sure until TJ underwent further examinations.

My heart sank again, but I could not let TJ see my concern. I had to remain stone-faced, confident-looking, and strong for him. I had to be his dad, his hero, his comfort in times when he is uncomfortable, the person who would tell him it was all going to be okay and he would believe it.

TJ had a red spot on his spine, the doctor explained, and that could be due to any one of three reasons: inflammation, an infection, or cancer. In the meantime, TJ could suit up for football because none of those reasons had to prevent him from playing. If it was inflammation, as long as TJ felt fine, he was good to go. The other more serious issues could not worsen with contact.

I reached out to Stephanie McMahon and Triple H to let them know what I just went through at the doctor's office. Stephanie immediately picked up the phone to talk to me. I cried. She assured me that all will be okay and told me she would do everything in her power to make sure we got whatever help we needed. That was followed up with a call from Vince McMahon asking if I needed anything and to keep him posted if I do. For him to call me on that particular day was big because it was a day of live TV, production meetings, and rehearsals, yet he took the time to break away from all of that. The McMahons are definitely great human beings. I'm positive I'm neither the first nor the last person to echo those sentiments.

TJ played that night, spectacularly.

I cheered him on, but it was hard to focus knowing what might be waiting for him in a few days.

As a WWE Global Ambassador, I'm often involved in bringing awareness to pediatric cancer. I've spent considerable time with children battling cancer. My Bullard Family Foundation gave $100,000 to Connor's Cure, a nonprofit first seeded by a $1-million donation from Stephanie McMahon and Triple H to fight cancer. Through a partnership between the V Foundation and WWE, Connor's Cure has raised around $4.5 million to fund research grants and provide family assistance, in the name of eight-year-old WWE fan Connor "The Crusher" Michalek, who lost his battle with cancer in 2014. Suddenly I might be on the other side of that battle, and I was numb.

Early the next week, TJ had his follow-up tests and was cleared. It was just inflammation. He was cancer free. Praise God. As fathers, our job is to protect and provide. That was the first time in my life I did not know how to fix a lot of things. It was the first time in my life I felt like there was nothing I could do. But the reality of it is that I did everything I should do, which was, first and foremost, pray and have faith that things would be okay regardless of what the previous misdiagnosis said. And then secondly, I utilized the resources that God had placed around me to help me get through the situation.

I understand I can do more for my family than a lot of people can. I had the resources and the connections to get my son those appointments. Otherwise, we could have possibly had to wait weeks for answers. And as a family, we would have had to sweat things out for much longer. And had the circumstances been different and it was cancer, while much of the outcome would have definitely been in God's hands, I also had the means to get TJ better treatment and care than most who have had to battle this horrible disease.

I will never give my kids everything they want, but I will give them much of what they want and always everything they need. I'm blessed and thankful I have the ability to do so. I will always provide my kids with the best of what that success has granted me.

Still, they are not spoiled, nor will they ever be.

How did they grow to become such unspoiled adults?

I will get to that later in this chapter.

———

My mom was a kid on her own, abandoned by her family, when she chose not to abort me. She did all she could on her own to raise me and my three brothers, who were fathered by another man who abandoned her and left her a single parent of four.

She had no high school education, no technical skills.

We lived in a Delray Beach neighborhood known as "The Hole" because those who lived there believed it was impossible to escape.

Drugs were everywhere. And crime was rampant.

We did not have birthday parties because we could not afford to have them. And while many believed in Santa Claus, I can assure you, jolly ol' St. Nick never visited our home. There was no heavyset white gentleman or Black gentleman coming down the chimney, eating cookies and milk because, number one, we did not have a chimney and, number two, if there were cookies to be eaten, I can assure you I ate them. I love cookies and I love milk so much I used to drink, at minimum, a gallon every other day.

Holidays did not mean as much to me as they may have to other families, although one holiday does stand out. I was 12 years old and I received a remote-controlled car from a woman at a Christmas charity event. She told me she had bought the car specifically for me. I thought, "There is no way this woman bought this car specifically for me—she doesn't even know me." But once I removed that negative thought, I replaced it with a positive one and immediately felt special. That remote-controlled car was probably the nicest gift I ever received as a child. It was fast, it did not have a string attached to it, and it was blue, my favorite color at the time. Most importantly, receiving something that was new and shiny provided me with dignity. I kept that car until my junior year of college, and I would still have that car to this day had it not been for my roommate at the time accidentally destroying it.

I still think about it from time to time. It was more than a car to me. It was one of the most significant gifts I ever received in my life. It imparted in me the value of ensuring the gifts I give are given with dignity. It also showed me what it looks like to provide someone with something that is not only special but also of value. Kids in underserved neighborhoods are so accustomed to receiving less than favorable items: hand-me-down clothes, recycled toys, government-program related services, the list goes on and on.

When it came to real cars, my mother always had access to one. Granted, it wasn't always in the best condition, and in a lot of cases, well, it was embarrassing, but it was a car. Sometimes it was a loaner from family or friends. Or, on the rare occasion that she was able to scrounge together a few hundred bucks to buy herself a car, it was what we call a beater because it was truly on its last legs. Getting out of her car was so embarrassing I would sometimes ask her to drop me off nearly a mile away from the destination.

In hindsight, regardless of the status or condition of the car that my mom had to drive, it still provided her with the ability to get to and from work at her convenience and not at the mercy of public transportation or rides from others.

It wasn't until I was a lot older that I appreciated and understood how much of a luxury it is to actually have a vehicle of any sort.

My father, Mr. Blalock, bought me my first car, a brand-new Hyundai Accent, while I was at the University of Florida. It was purple with three-star rims. You could not tell me nothing. I put 10-inch subwoofer speakers in it, which, as I sit here and think about, were way too much for that little car. It was a two-door car that had a front and back seat but could fit only two big bodies at the most. Whoever sat in the back definitely sat long ways. My teammates joked here and there about my car, but, in my eyes, the joke was truly on them. I had a set of four wheels that could get me where I wanted to go while they did not have a vehicle.

I had a great sense of pride knowing I could get on the road and go visit my dad in Live Oak or my mother in Delray Beach. It allowed me to get an off-campus apartment and still have the ability to get to campus, class, and football practice.

I'm not going to act as though I was a model young driver because I wasn't, especially when it came to parking. I might still hold the record for parking tickets and boot fees on the University of Florida campus. It's crazy I thought I could get away with it; my car wasn't in the least bit inconspicuous. It was probably the only purple car with three-star rims on the entire campus.

Looking at it glass half-full, all of those tickets did allow me to develop relationships with the on-campus police. And as time passed, because of the relationships, I received fewer tickets and phone calls telling me to move my car. I guess this was also an early lesson in building real connections and being a good person. I never cried or complained about getting the tickets; I recognized and understood I was the reason for the tickets on my windshield and the boots on my wheels.

My childhood was filled with trauma. But it was also filled with a lot of help from people, like the woman who gave me the remote-controlled car and my dad who gave me a real car. And that help has played a role in making me who I am. It's why I don't just serve one demographic of people. I serve all people.

My Bullard Family Foundation enjoys providing transportation to those in need. Over the past several years, the foundation has partnered with several different dealerships to provide dozens of families with a new car, debt free. These families, unsuspecting that they are about to have their lives changed through the gift of transportation, are always surprised with their new car. There are tons of success stories and happy moments. I will pick out two that stand out to me, both from 2020.

First, there was Virginia Lowell, better known as Miss Virginia to the students at the school that would later be named Thaddeus M. Bullard Academy at Sligh Middle Magnet School, where she had been employed as a cafeteria worker for 27 years. I presented a Publix gift card to the custodial and kitchen staffs as a token of my appreciation for what they did for the school. But, in partnership with Elder Ford, I had a special gift for Miss Virginia: a brand-new white Ford Escape to replace the beat-up Mitsubishi Lancer that she had been driving for years. She was 64 at the time, and it was the first new car she had ever driven. "God is good," she said and then took it for a spin around the football track at my school.

Next was the car I gave to Gabriel McClain and Larissa Lones, who were raising three children in New Port Richey.

With full-time jobs but no car, Gabriel and Larissa depended on others to get to work, to get their kids to school, and to run basic errands, like grocery shopping. They also felt limited in their job opportunities since they had to work at places that were easily accessible. So with the help of my friend Scott Fink, who owns Hyundai of New Port Richey, I gifted them a brand-new Hyundai Santa Fe. "We're beyond lucky, blessed is the word," Larissa said between tears.

Considering that I'm aware how important it is to own a car, considering my father bought me a car, and considering how much I enjoy giving cars to others, it should not shock you to learn I bought each of my kids whatever car they wanted. My kids will never know what it's like to pull up in a beater. I know friends who purposely buy their kids junk cars because, in their eyes, kids should be grateful for the fact that they even have transportation. I don't disagree with that outlook. To paraphrase Bobby Brown, that's their prerogative. But my prerogative is to give everyone my best, whether they are strangers, friends, or family. When I give to others, I don't give them anything that I wouldn't want to be seen in, eat, wear, or drive.

TJ's first car was a brand-new Nissan Maxima, which wasn't really his car per se because it was one that I received for free for promoting a dealership. But when they sold their business, I needed to turn in that vehicle so that they had it as part of their inventory. So now comes the harsh reality of how my kids have been raised. When I asked TJ what sort of car he wanted next, he said a BMW. And I thought, "What the . . . ?" But then he looked at me with his beautiful eyes and nice smile and put his hand on my shoulder and said, "You have always told us to ask for the best." That was Jedi mind tricking at its best and reverse psychology in motion. My inspirational words and way of life had backfired on me.

Well, I could not negate what I had preached nor the example I had set because I too only drive nice cars. Plus, again, I would not give my kids or others anything that I would not be willing to have myself. So, needless to say, TJ received his brand-new BMW.

As I write that last sentence, I think, "Damn, maybe my kids *are* spoiled." But I quickly remember that my kids are not spoiled. I spoil them, but they are not spoiled.

Next up for a new car was my daughter, Leah. She wanted a Kia Stinger, which I thought would be way more affordable. Nope. Not only was it one of the most difficult cars to find, but it was also one of the most expensive in the Kia collection. I thought to myself, "When in the hell did Kia become so expensive?" After further research, I realized it was a very fast sports car and thought, "Wait, Kia makes fast cars too?"

My daughter loves cars, so she knew every single aspect of this one. It was her dream car. She even knew the colors she wanted: black exterior with a red interior. And those colors made it even more difficult to find. There were only three or four for sale in the entire state. So I sent my friend Bob Murray from Ferman Ford down a rabbit hole, but he found the exact car my daughter wanted.

And then came the plot twist.

TJ had let my Leah drive his car a few times, which was enough for her to change her mind. She too wanted a BMW. Again, that thought: "Damn, maybe my kids *are* spoiled." No, they are not spoiled. I spoil them, but they are not spoiled.

I called Bob and explained that my daughter may be reconsidering her choice of cars. So we test-drove a few BMWs and then the Kia Stinger, which she chose. I'm not going to lie; it stung a little bit financially because the Kia had only three miles on it and the BMW had just under 600 miles. Bob had to work his magic on the deal, but he made it work.

And, finally, my third kid, Titus. He wanted a Ford Mustang Mach-E-GT. I did not know anything about that car either but, much like Leah did with her Kia, Titus knew it inside and out. Aside from a Lamborghini, he said, the Mach-E-GT was his dream car. I can assure you that I was not buying him a Lamborghini.

"Damn, maybe my kids *are* spoiled." No, my kids are not spoiled. I spoil them, but they are not spoiled.

So I went down another rabbit hole with my friend Bob Murray. Mind you, Titus had not turned 16 yet, which is the minimum driving age in Florida, nor would he be of age on Christmas when I planned on gifting him the car. But that was my plan anyway.

Wanting to avoid another Leah situation, I took him for a test-drive. Bob came too, so I had to squeeze my big frame into that back seat like my friends had to do in my college car. I felt helpless, nervous, scared, and every other synonym.

Bob guided him on the test-drive, telling him where to turn and where to go. And then Bob uttered ridiculous words that still haunt me to this day: "Step on it a little bit." That car has so much power, it whipped my neck back! "Titus, be careful!" I screamed as Bob laughed hysterically. He is a good son. He slowed down.

We finished the drive, and Bob proceeded to ask him, "Is this the car you want?" Mind you, I had no idea how much it cost. I had done zero research. But Titus did *all* the research, including the exterior and interior colors he wanted. Afterwards,

Titus and I took a picture with Bob. I have a look of disgust on my face. Titus looks ecstatic, knowing in his heart that he would end up with that car on his birthday. But that is not a surprise! That's why I planned on giving it to him on Christmas.

But he still had to prove he was worthy. Obviously, the big things mattered, like how he drove with his permit. If his foot was too heavy on that gas, he would get a figurative foot in the you know what by not getting a car that can drive as fast as the Mach-E-GT. But the little things mattered too, like how he kept his room. A sloppy room means a sloppy car, and I wasn't going to gift him something that expensive just for him to ruin.

He passed all my tests, so it was time to surprise him on Christmas Day.

I parked the car in a neighbor's garage weeks before Christmas and then distracted him that afternoon with games of Ping-Pong. Of course, I'm the Ping-Pong champion in my house and never waver on the winner-stays-on rule. But I made an exception that day and let TJ stay on to play Titus, even though I had just kicked his butt. I worried Titus might realize something was up when I did so, but he suspected nothing.

I had friends gather around the table to create a Super Bowl atmosphere for their game and to keep Titus fully engaged while I slipped away to pull the car into the driveway. I then yelled for Titus to come to the front of the house to meet someone. And when he saw that car, he lost his mind. He ran up and down the neighborhood screaming, "I can't believe it! I can't believe it!" while stopping to hug everyone he could. Finally, my friend Ray looked at Titus and, with a laugh, asked, "Are you going to thank your father?" to which my son responded with his strongest hug ever.

And then came the first drive. I immediately thought to myself, "I regret this decision." It had *so much* pickup . . .

That night, as I looked out my window at another brand-new car sitting in my driveway, I thought to myself, "Damn, my kids are spoiled."

Then I realized they are not in the least.

———

Game 6 of the 2019 NBA Finals was one of the greatest professional basketball games I have ever witnessed.

1. There was history. It resulted in the first NBA title in the then-26-year history of the Toronto Raptors, courtesy of an iconic season by Kawhi Leonard.

2. There was heartbreak. Klay Thompson tore his left ACL at the 2:22 mark of the third quarter, just one game after Kevin Durant ruptured his Achilles tendon.

3. There was excitement. During the course of four quarters, there were 18 lead changes and nine ties before the Raptors held on for a 114–100 victory.

4. There was a goodbye. It was the final game at the Oracle Arena. Even in defeat, Golden State fans left the arena screaming "WARRIORS" one last time. And, admit it, if you know basketball, you chanted "WARRIORS" multiple times.

And I was there, in seats near the floor, to witness it all with my sons. I bought the tickets the moment both teams punched their ticket to the finals. One son was a big time Kawhi fan that season. The other loved the Dubs.

Offers came pouring in as friends learned I had tickets to that coveted game. I was offered a ludicrous amount of money to part with my tickets. LUDICROUS! And, yes, for a moment, I did consider selling them and taking my sons for wings instead, but I didn't do it, even as friends upped their offers. The Million Dollar Man Ted DiBiase was wrong, I guess. Not everyone has a price. I knew it would be an experience that my sons would never forget. For me, memories and moments are more valuable than money. And as we stood on the floor next to Raptors Superfan Nav Bhatia, I knew I had made the right decision.

I went to just one professional sporting event as a kid. The Girls and Boys Club took a group of us to a Miami Dolphins game. We had good seats too—second level near an end zone. I recall being mesmerized by the size of the stadium, the sound of the crowd, and the speed of the game. As we walked out, I couldn't wait to watch another football game in a stadium.

It would be nearly a decade before I was at another.

Mr. Blalock made trips to watch Florida A&M football games a regular part of our lives. While there were many others in Live Oak who offered to take me to Florida State games, Mr. Blalock insisted that I go with him to Florida A&M games. I guess it was because of his innate hatred toward the Florida State Seminoles.

I will never forget the first one we attended. It was FAMU's homecoming, and I was more struck by their marching band, perhaps the best in the world, than the football action. That's not a slight on the team; it's high praise for the marching band.

That trip was memorable for so many reasons. It was my first father-son trip outside of Live Oak with Mr. Blalock. It was the first college football game I ever attended. It was my first ever FAMU homecoming. And, finally, it was the first time I called Mr. Blalock Dad and asked him if it was okay to do so. He said absolutely, as long as he could call me his son.

Those games provided memories I will never forget.

And that's why it's important for me to help others create their own memories at live sporting and entertainment events.

In 2018, as a member of the Gasparilla Bowl Executive Committee, I helped 10,000 Tampa Bay–area kids get tickets to see the Marshall Thundering Herd take on the University of South Florida at the Gasparilla Bowl at Raymond James Stadium. The smiles on those kids' faces going into the stadium and during the game showed that they were having the time of their lives and creating memories of a lifetime. Unfortunately, the University of South Florida Bulls lost. But it was still a great day for these children.

And creating memories for and with my kids is why I take them to so many live events. They have been to college football national championships, Stanley Cup games, Super Bowls, and, as already mentioned, the NBA Finals. They have seen some of the greatest artists live in concert, including Meek Mill, Drake, Kendrick Lamar, Migos, and so many others. They met celebrities and even have befriended some, such as Flo Rida, Snoop Dogg, Kevin Durant, Saquon Barkley, and, of course, Dave Bautista, whom we consider family.

Name a big-time live event, and they have likely attended, sometimes numerous times, or will likely do so in the future.

Enjoying a family trip to Raymond James Stadium. Go Bucs!

Leah and me on a recruiting visit at South Carolina State. Leah ultimately signed to Oakland University on a full basketball scholarship.

Stopping for a family photo just before *Royal Rumble* in our hometown, Tampa, FL.

Father's Day 2023 at a steakhouse in Tampa with my three beautiful kids. I am truly blessed.

At home, TJ poses with Leah, who is ready to play with some WWE figures.

Titus joined me for a screening of the movie *Air*. We hosted 140 families from our community, which is something I do quite frequently.

Leah is successful in her championship semifinal game in 2023.

Visiting Dave at his tattoo shop, DC Society Ink. Leah and I left with matching tattoos!

Dave and I support the boys during TJ's Senior Night at Berkley Prep.

Hanging with Leah and our dog Frazier in the backyard. You know our yard is decked with a Gators logo!

The whole family is on hand at *WrestleMania 38* in Dallas, TX.

All smiles after Titus signs with my alma mater, the University of Florida. Dave joined us for a celebratory dinner.

Yes, sometimes I spoil my kids. Here I am surprising Titus with a Mustang on Christmas morning, 2022.

TJ and me hanging out with Uncle Dave. Huge appetites all around!

Leah and I accompany Titus on a visit to the University of Florida. This is the Gators' indoor practice facility.

Proud dad moment as Leah captures her astounding fifth state championship for varsity basketball.

TJ looks sharp at his graduation from Berkley Prep! Titus shows his support repping UCF, where TJ will enroll and join the football team.

Holding TJ shortly after bringing him home. This is our first photo shoot together.

Offering Titus some fatherly advice at his high school graduation. He knows how proud I am.

I love spending time with my kids. I love being their dad. I'm not in the least bit apologetic for this.

But, yes, the word *spoil* was always in the back of my mind early on. Was I giving them too much? Were they going to appreciate going anywhere if they went everywhere?

I have since learned they did appreciate what I was giving them and they know they lived blessed lives.

Perhaps it could be said that I spoil my children.

But they are certainly not spoiled.

———

There is a difference between spoiling your children and raising spoiled children.

Giving your children things, taking them places, providing them with opportunities is not how a child becomes spoiled.

Not providing them with values is how children become spoiled. It's really that simple.

Raise your kids right. That is all it takes.

I have rules that I expect my children to follow.

1. Love and respect everyone you come in contact with. You are not always going to agree with them. On some occasions, you might not even like them. But you always love them and respect them.

2. Be your best. If your best is a C on a test, even if it's a D or an F, neither you nor I can be disappointed if you gave it your all. Hard work doesn't always lead to victory, but it always brings success if you bring the best version of yourself. It's when you know, for

a fact, that you could have studied harder, trained more, or worked smarter that you can truly find the greatest disappointment. You never want to put yourself in a position where you say to yourself, "If I just would have . . ."

3. We don't use the word *can't*. It's not in our vocabulary. Throughout my entire childhood, I was told I would never amount to anything. For some people, when you tell them what they can't do, that's what drives them. They look at you and think, "You are not going to tell me what I can and cannot do. You are not going to define my limitations." But for others, those words can be the final straw that breaks their spirit. So even if my kids come to me with the most outrageous idea, I never tell them that I don't think they can pull that off. Instead, we sit down and figure out what needs to be achieved to get it done in the end.

4. Pay it forward. People invested in me at a young age when they had nothing to gain in return. I come from a single parent home, and my mom was a very, very young parent. Had it not been for the kindness and love and care of people at the Florida Sheriffs Youth Ranch, I would not be in the position that I'm in today. The more successful I become, the more opportunities I have to do more for people in the community and to repay the investment that people made in me when they did not have to.

5. I tell my kids all the time: "Don't be like me. Be better than me." Sometimes parents tell their kids

to do one thing and then do the complete opposite. That's confusing. How can I expect my children to respect and love other people if they don't see me doing that?

6. See the world. Don't isolate yourself to the neighborhood you live in, the school you attend, or the sports you play. Expose yourself to various aspects of life, even if your life doesn't include the blessings or shortcomings of others. Our differences should not be our dividers.

7. Help whomever you can. A while back, I met a boy with cancer named Logan Larrabee, a huge WWE fan who wanted to meet a WWE Superstar. I ended up staying with Logan for three hours. Then four hours after I left, he passed away. I have never lost a child, so when his father called me, I asked if there was anything I could do. Logan had three brothers, so I took the boys to the movies and invited them over to play in the pool and stay the night while their parents made funeral arrangements. We are all still friends to this day.

8. Stay humble. I'm accustomed to sharing because when I was a kid, family was all that we had. We had to learn how to live off little. We lived in an apartment in the projects and, at times, did not have much food. There is nothing wrong with coming from humble beginnings. It's remaining humble and remembering where you came from that's important. When you are walking past people who live on the street, rather

than shying away from them, hug them, tell them hello, or pray for them.

My kids hear these rules so often, even now as young adults, they can rattle them off, almost verbatim to how I wrote them. They are ingrained in their minds and souls and are their way of life. These eight rules lead near every decision that my kids make.

We were in Brooklyn one summer and passed by a homeless man on our walk from our nice hotel to the nice restaurant where we were going for breakfast. We ate a delicious meal and then, before we left, I ordered a breakfast to go and gave it to that homeless man on our walk back to our hotel. As my son recalls it, there were no fans around. There were no television cameras or reporters. I did not take a picture with the man and post the story on social media. I just did it because it was the right thing to do.

Back home in Tampa, both sons were always by my side at my Joy of Giving and Back to School Bash events, hard at work too. They would sort presents, help with inventory, set up, clean up, and break down. They would also recruit their teammates and friends to participate. And they have joined me at Metropolitan Ministries on Thanksgiving and Christmas mornings to help prepare meals to serve to the less fortunate and have also helped me throughout the year to spread joy at nursing homes and pediatric hospitals.

I have always strived to set an example for my children that reminds them that our family is better off than many.

Words matter. Those rules that I preach matter. But actions speak louder than words.

There were certainly times when my sons were little that I felt they did not understand or appreciate what they were given.

They would ask me for money to go to the movies, just days after I gave them an allowance. I would ask what happened to all their money, and they would say that they bought new sneakers or clothes or something like that. That is great, I would say back, but you should have saved some of that money for the movies, so tell your friends you will catch up with them at the next one.

I saw my lessons seeping through when they were around 12 or 13. They would make a friend or get a new teammate whose shoes were talking or clothes were tattered, as mine were as a kid, and they would ask if we could help through our Bullard Family Foundation. Or they would ask for money for the movies and tell me they used their allowance to buy new shoes for a kid who could not afford a pair or food for a hungry family. I would instantly smile and then proceed to give them money so they could enjoy themselves.

I'm proud of my children, and I tell them that regularly, and they equally share that sentiment with me.

———

Providing for my kids is not just about material items. It's also about mental and physical health.

All three kids have been going to personal trainers for years. They have each been subscribed to a meal prep program so they can eat healthy food on days when we don't have time to prepare a meal on our own. They do the same regimen as I do when it comes to taking care of their bodies. They have regular chiropractic visits and massages to keep their bodies in tune, and they have access to therapists to address mental health problems whenever they need.

But with all of these supports readily available to them, I have always demanded accountability.

For example, time is the only asset that can't be increased. My kids know how I feel about time. If I was taking them to the gym or to the movies or dinner, and they knew we left at 5:30 in the morning or evening, they were expected to be waiting at that front door by 5:15 because I pull out of that driveway at 5:30 sharp. I did not care if I saw them exiting the house as I pulled out of the driveway. I kept going without them. In my mind, they were late and there is no excuse for such behavior.

Some people might call this cruel. I call this a lesson—a very hard lesson. As their parent, it's not my job to always be the fun and beloved father. My job is to prepare them for the real world. If they are late to a job or class, even by a minute, that might sit wrong with their boss or teachers.

They need to be respectful of my time. They need to be respectful of everyone's time. Because not doing so means they are not thinking about anyone else but themselves. If you act like the world revolves around your schedule, that selfish way of thinking will ultimately lead to your destruction and people labeling you as spoiled.

I'm proud that my kids are consistently on time. No, they are not perfect, and there are times that they are late for reasons beyond their control, but they are very aware of how that impacts others.

And I'm proud that they are always aware that their every action might impact someone else.

I proudly say both of my sons worked while in high school.

TJ was first a cashier at a restaurant chain called PDQ and later collected carts at Publix, a local grocery store. Titus worked at a summer camp.

Through those jobs, they learned the value of a dollar. I noticed that they bought fewer shoes and clothes when they had to use their own money. Funny how that works. They learned the value of hard work.

Through those jobs, they further learned that the world doesn't revolve around them. They learned that they had to be part of a team and take orders from those above them on the corporate food chain.

TJ, the first of the two to get a job, promised to give me a cut of his first check as a thank you for all the money I had spent on him. He did the math in his head and knew what he could afford to give me. But he forgot about taxes.

The check was $86.

Later that day, I received a text from TJ: "Got my check. Going to Venmo you $10. Don't spend it all at once, please."

Here is what is most important: I did not demand that they get jobs. I did not even ask them to get jobs. They wanted to do so on their own.

They saw how hard I worked to provide for them and wanted to provide for themselves, despite knowing that they could remain unemployed teenagers and still have more than most.

I also did not ask them to help with their car payments, but they do when they can.

Yes, I might spoil my kids with great things, but they are not definitely spoiled.

CHAPTER 8

BLACK FATHERS, BLACK CHILDREN

When it comes to raising children, it's important to recognize there is a wide range of experiences and not all fathers encounter the same obstacles.

I cannot speak of how race impacts fathers who are white, Asian, or Latino. My experiences are as a Black father, so this chapter can focus only on that point of view. I would gladly sit down with fathers of any race to learn more about their experiences. I hope that by sharing my experiences, we can begin to better understand one another.

So let's talk about race, racism, parenting, and raising Black children in the United States.

But first, let's be clear. I'm not anti–law enforcement. I never have been; I never will be.

Law enforcement has positively impacted my life in various ways.

As a troubled young man, the Florida Sheriffs Youth Ranch literally helped save my life.

And I can genuinely say that my adult experiences with law enforcement have almost entirely been positive. I have worked with law enforcement agencies to establish community projects on many occasions.

I attest and stand by this: the vast majority of law enforcement officers who take the oath are very good people who are honored to serve their communities.

If a teacher goes out and does something heinous, that doesn't make all teachers bad. If a doctor performs malpractice, that doesn't make all doctors bad. If a coach does something inappropriate to a player, it doesn't make all coaches bad. The same goes for law enforcement.

But I can also say that our justice system and the culture within law enforcement has not been fair to people of color.

With all that said, let's talk about "The Talk."

For most parents, "The Talk" is when parents discuss sex with their children for the first time. But for Black parents, "The Talk" has a second meaning.

Make no mistake about it, I have always been aware of the racial divide, even at a young age. Anyone of color who grew up in an underprivileged neighborhood can likely say the same.

Substance use and alcohol were prevalent in my community. I often saw Black men and women drunk and high out in the street. I don't condone them being intoxicated or high in public, or in private for that matter; drugs and alcohol are not my thing, but to each their own. I equally do not approve of the ways that law enforcement officers chose to deal with these individuals in my neighborhood.

There were times when law enforcement was a little too rough. There were times when they were seemingly very disrespectful.

And there were times when they violently arrested people while children were present. I'm sure there were many situations that looked like the Wild West when it came to law enforcement and people in my community.

Looking back, many of those people who used substances or alcohol would have benefited more by receiving mental health counseling than being placed behind prison bars. So when people were calling for police departments to be defunded, I did not agree. I think more funds should be contributed in order to hire professionals who know how to deal with mental health problems.

Due to what we witnessed and experienced, many children and adults in my community feared law enforcement but did not respect them.

When Coach Bump, my childhood football coach and a Black police officer, overheard my teammates and me talking down law enforcement, he did not get angry that we were speaking poorly about those he served with. Instead, he gathered us up and spoke to us from his well-rounded point of view.

Yes, Coach Bump told us, there are some bad police officers out there, and yes, those men and women will mentally convict us due to the color of our skin. But, he said, it's wrong for us to say that all law enforcement officers are evil and against us, and we cannot treat them as the enemy. At some point, we will need their protection or assistance.

Unfortunately, he said, as Black men, especially Black football players who have size to them, it is best to approach every officer with caution until we learn which type they are. Remain calm, be respectful and not a smart ass, and always do all you can to safely get home.

That's "The Talk."

My dad, Mr. Blalock, almost learned the hard way what happens when a young Black man doesn't heed the lessons of "The Talk."

While he was a student at Florida A&M University, a law enforcement officer driving in front of my father slammed on the brakes to pull him over. "Turn your ignition back on and put your foot on the brake, *boy*," the officer demanded.

My dad did as he was told, and the officer informed him that he had been pulled over for a bad brake light.

"That is pretty amazing," my dad said. "You must be a psychic to have known that I had a bad brake light while driving in front of me like that."

Well, that did not go over well. The officer returned to his car, called for backup, and took my father to a police station.

His dad posted the $50 bail, but the officers waited more than an hour to release him. On my dad's way out, an officer told him that he needed to learn how to talk to white people. My dad replied, "Well, I'm a college student. I will take that class next semester."

But my dad wasn't in a joking mood.

He drove straight home, went between his mother's mattresses, and grabbed a pistol with the intent to return to that police station and teach those officers a lesson.

His father was unable to stop him, but being an important man in Perry, he called some of his white law enforcement friends for help. One of those friends pulled Dad over, took pistol shotgun, and brought him back home.

If not for that save, who knows what would have happened.

His father then advised him, "Son, you need to learn to take abuse, move on, and channel that anger for good."

My father took that to heart and joined the civil rights movement in Tallahassee.

He was arrested for using a whites-only drinking fountain, for sitting at a whites-only lunch counter, and for trying to buy a ticket at a whites-only movie theater, each time taking the abuse and using it as motivation.

When recalling those times to me, he always reminded me of what someone told him at a Dr. Martin Luther King Jr. rally in Tallahassee. "If you cannot stand to be called a n***er, if you cannot stand to be kicked and spit on, then don't join the cause. It takes physical strength to protect yourself. It takes mental strength to change the country."

That is not always part of "The Talk," but it needs to be.

My father taught that lesson to me. I then taught it to my children.

———

This chapter was supposed to only be about raising Black children and that is what I set out to focus on.

I wanted to write about the gross stereotype that all Black fathers are absentee fathers. I take that stereotype personal considering I'm very active and involved in raising my children, as are all of my Black friends. Yes, there are absentee Black fathers in this nation. But there are also absentee white fathers, Latino fathers, Asian fathers, and so on. So why is that stereotype placed primarily on Black fathers?

In this chapter, I wanted to write about socioeconomic inequalities in the United States. Disparities like a lack of educational opportunities and income inequality can make it more difficult for a Black father to provide for his children.

I wanted to write about the disproportionate incarceration of Black fathers and the limited positive representation of Black fathers in the media.

In this chapter, I wanted to educate people from all races on what it is like to be a Black father, as I did by writing about "The Talk."

Then I realized that many may not believe my words no matter how convincing they are, so I needed to go another route.

I recall sitting in my car after the death of George Floyd, looking at pictures of my children and breaking into tears. As a Black father, it's frustrating, hurtful, scary. I've been able to teach my kids a lot about life, but I'm not equipped to teach or tell my kids or other Black children how to deal with this type of crap over and over and over again. I realized there are many people in this country who don't believe that we as a nation need to address why what happened to George Floyd seems to happen to other Black men and women time and again. And then I realized they don't believe it needs to be addressed because they refuse to listen. They hear the words but block out the message.

I realized that it's not enough for me to raise my Black children right if everyone doesn't raise their children right.

It's equally not enough for a Jewish or Mexican father to raise his children right if everyone doesn't raise their children right.

We cannot end racism until we are all willing to listen to one another.

We cannot raise better people until we become better people.

We cannot properly raise any child of any race right if we as adults don't understand right from wrong. And being able to understand right from wrong starts with knowing the real issues that others face.

So let's focus on opening the minds of all parents, so they can then open their children's minds. If you are uncomfortable discussing this, then you are the person who needs to read this the most.

Everybody—and I'm talking about everybody, whether it affects you directly or not—needs to stand up and face it, even if it's uncomfortable, because until we start putting it all on the table and discussing it, it's never going to change.

Some of you go to sporting events or concerts or live events all the time, even when it's uncomfortable. You don't care about the weather, where you must park, or where you are sitting. You make a conscious effort to get to that event because you are invested.

Well, it's time for all of us to become interested and invested in recognizing the differences in our races and the stereotypes we each must deal with. Be willing to be uncomfortable. Be willing to ask questions and give answers. Don't brush aside people's hurt and anger. Having conversations can lead people to see things and learn things about other cultures.

One example: early in his high school career, TJ and a few of his friends were playing around in the hallway when a teacher approached. The kids were not being destructive or obscene or doing drugs or anything like that, but they were being a bit playfully rowdy, and the teacher had every right to confront them. But the way the teacher chose to address them, right out of the gate, was problematic.

"Quit monkeying around," screamed the teacher, who was white.

TJ's white friends did not take offense to that. But TJ and his Black friends did.

A monkey is not just a monkey to a Black person. Monkey is also a racial slur.

It's the same with the word "boy." You will never hear me refer to Black children as boys. They are always "young men." "Boy" is a derogatory term that racists use to put Black men in their place. "Do your job, boy." "Keep quiet, boy."

I said something to the school about the monkey comment, and some of the white parents did not understand why we were offended and why the teacher needed to be told to cut that phrase out of their vocabulary.

Privilege would never see this as a problem.

I believe that the majority of racist comments are not malicious. They are just uninformed and not well thought-out. It's okay to make a linguistic mistake, apologize, and move on, as long as you listen to why it offends someone. I don't even expect you to understand why. Someone who is not Black can in no way understand what it's like to be a Black person in America, just as I could not understand what it's like to be a Jewish person. But everyone needs to understand that people are treated differently. That means people will react differently to certain things. So while you may not mean to offend a person of another race, when that person tells you that it was offensive, instead of getting upset about it and telling them to toughen up or trying to sweep it under the rug, take the time to listen to why that person is insulted.

I can assure you that no one in the Black community wants to protest anymore. We don't want to sit our kids down for "The Talk" again and again. Quite frankly, we are tired of it. We just want this to end.

If a person says Black lives matter and your immediate response is anything but agreement, then you are not listening.

If you must scream back that all lives matter, you are not listening. No one has ever said that your life doesn't matter. We are saying that there are many people in this country who don't think that Black lives matter and that needs to change. I agree. All lives do matter, but all lives have not been treated the same in this country. All lives don't lead this nation in mass incarceration. All lives are not being shot at for jogging through a white neighborhood.

I have many friends from many different races. When talking about race and race issues with some of my white friends, they stand on the fact that they don't see color. I immediately correct them and say, "Well, if you don't see color, you don't see my race. If you don't see my race, then you could care less about the issues my race must deal with on a day-to-day basis. And that means we can never have an honest conversation about how to bring everyone in this nation together."

If I'm offended by something that you said, like *monkeying around* or *boy*, don't tell me that my skin is too thin. Don't tell me that words don't matter. Don't tell me how to feel as a Black man and father in America.

Instead, ask me why I feel that way and understand that your words can hurt.

And if I say something that offends you, let me know. Again, I cannot understand what it is like to be a father of another race, creed, or color other than my own. Educate me. I promise that I will listen.

To my fellow Black fathers, this must work both ways. If someone says something that offends you as a Black man, just getting angry and screaming "racist" at the perpetrator is not the solution. Remain calm and attempt to explain why you were offended. Try to open a mind before opening your mouth to scream.

That is how we can start to heal as a nation.

It starts with acceptance of truth. Our kids, grandkids, brothers, sisters, mothers, and fathers are not telling and have not been telling lies. Our truth needs to be addressed. It's then that "WE" can change the world. When "ME" becomes "WE," amazing things can and will happen.

———

Some years back, WWE asked me to write about what Black History Month means to me.

While the ages of my children and the mentions of movies are outdated, the sentiment is timeless, so I would like to share it here:

> *Black History Month is upon us, and many use this time to honor African Americans for their contributions to American culture. I support Black History Month in its concerted effort to spotlight African Americans and their many significant accomplishments; however, while some might solely recognize Black history in February, our history is celebrated every day in my home.*
>
> *My goal is to not only use African American history to help instill pride in my children, but to also celebrate diversity without perpetuating a divide. Our culture's remarkable, rich, and vibrant stories are crucial to America's development and balance. My hope is that one day, America will not need a*

designated month to focus on African Americans' place in history. Instead, our history will be taught as one with all of American history.

I take the responsibility of sharing with my sons the struggles, triumphs, and feats of their fellow African Americans year-round. I recently took my two sons to watch Selma, a movie about Dr. Martin Luther King Jr.'s campaign to secure equal voting rights and the historic marches from Selma, Ala., to Montgomery. At the ages 10 and eight, my sons have also seen Amistad, 42: The Jackie Robinson Story, Ali, and other movies that address Black history. I expose them to literature, music, and history in all forms so they can see the beauty and strength of their culture's background.

I'm grateful that, personally and professionally, I have had the opportunity to impact people of all races and to show them that hard work and dedication can produce greatness. I strive to be an example of how someone can overcome a challenging childhood and succeed regardless of obstacles or negative environments. Teaching our youth how to stay true to their values, to embrace diversity, and to recognize their own gifts is vital to helping future generations achieve and promote racial equality. By using these measures in my early years, I was able to attain a confident mindset and not be afraid to accept help from outside my community.

I have had the privilege of serving as an ambassador for WWE's community and outreach initiatives in the United States and around the world. As an ambassador, I have been part of WWE's campaign to promote literacy as well as its anti-bullying program, Be a STAR (Show Tolerance and Respect). I have also had the honor of being featured in the Ad Council and U.S. Department of Health and Human Services Fatherhood campaign that encourages dads to recognize their critical role and gives them the tools to help get more involved.

I recognize that I have become a role model to many during my time with WWE. I have role models who I look up to and who have deeply impacted my life too. I have enjoyed learning about the past efforts of our global humanitarian leaders, like Dr. Martin Luther King Jr., Muhammad Ali, and Rev. Jesse Jackson. They are legendary contributors to American history. Recently, I was honored as the 2014 Rainbow PUSH Coalition's humanitarian awardee. This is of great relevance to me and a momentous blessing. Rev. Jesse Jackson's Rainbow PUSH Coalition is dedicated to social equality, reading programs, and job placement for our youth. It provides a vast array of beneficial programs to promote African-Americans' success and positive race relations.

This distinction was also given to Ali, Maya Angelou, and Jackie Robinson in the past. Since being given that award, I have become friends with Rev. Jackson, a key figure of the civil rights movement who worked alongside Dr. King and many other courageous leaders. It was an indescribable moment, and it deepened my connection and appreciation for our culture's history. That appreciation is something I hope to pass down to my children and the children I hope to inspire.

My greatest hope is that my words and actions help future generations see the light in themselves, regardless of their background, current circumstances, or race. When I step into the ring for WWE, my purpose is to entertain and to inspire everyone. I want children and adults to see me as an entertainer, one that they enjoy booing or cheering, based on my talents as a performer and not the color of my skin. Dreams can be accomplished by anyone with the courage to follow them. I do my best to inspire everyone to "reach for the moon because if they fail, they'll land on the stars."

America is one of the most diverse countries in the world, a true melting pot. People from all races, ethnicities, religions, and beliefs made this country what it is today. The more educated we are about our people and cultures, the more understanding we possess and the more aware we are of how to improve ourselves. We must remember "we were all humans until race disconnected us, religion separated us, politics divided us, and wealth classified us." Let's use our differences to teach instead of divide. Let's remember that we all share history as humans. So, in honor of Black History Month, this human will end this blog by saying it loud: "I'm Black, and I'm proud!"

In Tampa, as part of Black History Month, we often recall the tragedy of Martin Chambers.

On June 11, 1967, three young Black men were racing from a photo store and through the Central Park Village housing projects, each allegedly with handfuls of stolen goods.

The trio split up and, again allegedly, each dropped the photo equipment that they had supposedly stolen.

One of the young men later admitted that he broke into the photo store and acted alone. Another of the young men said that the three of them robbed it together. The third young man, Martin Chambers, all of 19 years old at the time, never had the opportunity to tell his side of the story.

An officer spotted Chambers and, knowing he was a suspect in the robbery of a whopping $100 of photo equipment, fired his gun at the young man from 25 yards away. The officer said he aimed for Chambers's right shoulder and accidentally shot the young man in the back. The bullet then passed through Chambers's chest, killing him.

Later, Tampa's Black community spilled into the streets of the entertainment district of Central Avenue, some in peaceful protest, but seemingly more to riot.

By the time it was calmed, more than 500 Florida National Guardsmen, nearly 250 Florida Highway Patrolmen, and around 250 local law enforcement officers were brought in to bring order to the city.

The officer wasn't charged with a crime.

Black history is still being written. Someday, these recent years of debate and strife will be included in Black History Month.

In the days following the death of George Floyd, like most cities in the United States, Tampa was host to a number of protests. They were organized as peaceful, but one night, a protest turned violent when a Champs Sports store was looted and lit on fire and a neighboring SunTrust Bank branch was damaged.

The next day, as expected, many no longer wanted to talk about George Floyd or how Black lives matter.

Nobody is going to listen to a person or a group of people when they are acting like that. Many instead turn their attention to the violence perpetrated by a few members of the community. We need to learn how to control our anger and apply, strategize, mobilize, and get people from all walks of life moving in the same direction.

We need to stop tearing down our community. Rioting is not going to solve anything. There are people who are going to sit back and laugh and say, "Aha, what did I tell you, they're animals."

Don't complain if you are contributing to the violence and are part of the problem. Be a solution and a positive example of what not to do to the community and especially to your children.

I'm not in favor of people rioting and looting. I'm in favor of people coming together and taking a stand. That is exactly what we need to do as a community. And it's what we need to do as a country.

I just want to live in a world where lives that historically did not matter now do and voices are heard by people who have been deaf for far too long.

In response to the looting, the Tampa Police Department, City of Tampa, and Hillsborough Sheriff's Office held a press conference to ask for calm. They allowed me to speak.

"I understand that people are out there, are hurting and upset and mad. I'm mad as hell . . . but this happened in Minnesota, not in Tampa, Florida," I said.

"What's your angle?" I later asked. "That is what I would ask any protester out there. What is your angle? This happened in Minnesota. All right? How can we take what happened in Minnesota and bring it to Tampa and figure out a way to build relationships with law enforcement and hold them accountable?"

To the looters, I said, "Enough is enough. You cannot clean up somebody else's house when your house is dirty. We have a great reputation of being a great city here in Tampa, with great leadership. This is not the way to do it."

But words were not enough for me. I wanted to follow those up with actions.

So a few days later, I led a "Love Walk" to promote racial equality and justice. I wanted my walk to be different than the others occurring throughout my community.

The others seemed to focus on anger. While they had every right to be angry, I wondered if those walks were going to have a positive impact. They were speaking out against racism, local law enforcement, and locally elected officials. But I felt that some were putting everyone in one basket and considering everyone in those groups as part of the problem. Instead, they needed to point out that the bad cops throughout the country are a minority. They needed to say that we must do a better job of weeding out those who cannot be trusted in such positions of power and that we must find better ways to hold them accountable.

Erroneously putting everyone in one basket, I worried, threatened to further the divide between law enforcement and the Black community.

I hoped that my 90-minute civil rights walk could bridge that divide. To do so, I looked to the past.

My friend David Bautista joined me, as did the current Tampa mayor and former police chief Jane Castor. We asked that everyone remain positive and focus on discussing solutions and not anger. If I heard someone scream in anger, I spoke with them and asked that they voice their issues in a calm, level-headed manner. Get rid of the hate, I told them, before it consumes you.

We started at downtown Tampa's Curtis Hixon Waterfront Park and walked across the nearby Madame Fortune Taylor Bridge, named for a former enslaved woman who, in the years following emancipation, owned 33 acres of Tampa land along the Hillsborough River.

That bridge named in honor of a Black female property owner, I believed, proved what was possible, even in those violently racist years following the Civil War.

We ended at Julian B. Lane Riverfront Park, named for the white Tampa mayor who, in 1960, listened to the city's Black students who held sit-ins at white lunch counters. That mayor then brought together civil rights leaders, elected officials, and downtown business owners and worked to desegregate city eateries.

That is historical proof that when we come together, we can find solutions.

Perhaps my co-organizer, University of South Florida's then–senior cornerback KJ Sails, made the most symbolic gesture when he invoked the name of Martin Chambers during the walk.

Despite the heavy presence of law enforcement in the days that followed the death of Chambers, they had little to do with ending the violence. Instead, that credit went to the Black community.

Civil rights activists approached law enforcement leaders and let them know that the Black community would not respond well to police and the military marching into their neighborhoods. Instead, they recommended forming a citizen force made up entirely of the Black community. Law enforcement was weary of that suggestion but figured they had nothing to lose, so gave it the okay.

More than 100 young Black men were recruited to the cause, with each being given a white helmet to distinguish themselves. Those "White Hats," as they were called, then walked through the Black neighborhoods and asked that everyone remain calm. They reminded the community that the best way to make change was to work to change the system, rather than to break it.

In the following years, the city hired the first Black firefighters, the first Black assistant city attorney, the first Black secretary in the mayor's office, and the first Black head of the Tampa Housing Authority. In 1969, as many as 60 additional African Americans were hired by the city government for administrative jobs.

To parents of all colors: the solution to racism, the solution to raising a child of any race in America, is for people of all colors and races to teach their children to love and respect everyone.

If we work together, we can truly make this the greatest country in the world.

CHAPTER 9

BEING A SPORTS PARENT

A t the time that I write this, a little more than 20,000 men have ever stepped on a Major League Baseball diamond, just under 5,000 men have heard their sneakers squeak on the court as part of the National Basketball Association, around 25,000 men have stepped onto the gridiron for the National Football League, and nearly 8,000 men have skated on the ice for the National Hockey League.

Raymond James Stadium, where my hometown Tampa Bay Buccaneers play, can seat 65,000 fans.

So to put your child's chances of becoming a professional athlete in perspective: if you gave a free Buccaneers ticket to every man who has ever played for one of the United States' four major professional sports leagues, they still could not sell out a game.

———

It was the summer after his junior year of high school in Perry, Florida, when my father, Mr. Blalock, got an itch for a better summer job. Friends of his worked at a local farm picking tobacco and watermelon and, on Friday and Saturday nights, always seemed to have four times more money than he did. My dad wanted to join them in the fields, but for weeks his mother replied with a stern "No."

"You always seem to get into trouble," she told him. "Trouble just finds you, and there are probably a lot of opportunities for trouble at that farm."

But my dad wore her down through constant pleas. She finally caved and let him join his friends.

The adult men were professionals in the tobacco field. They were quick and strong when it came to picking and had flawless technique. They gave my dad a quick lesson and then ran off to get to work themselves. They were paid depending on how much they picked and did not want to waste too much time on a kid who was only there for summer work.

Well, my father fell behind and was bringing up the rear, which annoyed one of the white employees who my dad figured was a boss or owned the farm. "Catch up, you n***er," he kept yelling to my dad. "Stop being such a lazy n***er." Each racial slur that flew from that guy's mouth further agitated my dad, but that man was the boss, he figured, so he just had to take it, swallow hard, and deal.

During the mid-morning break, my dad asked the other Black employees how they dealt with a boss like that. "He is not the boss," they laughed. "He is not the payoff man. He is just a straw boss. He doesn't own the place." Not the boss? He was just some racist guy who thought he could speak to a young Black man any way he pleased? My dad saw stars.

Once back to work, that straw boss started on my dad again.

"Catch up, n***er," he spat at my dad.

"Catch up your damn self," my dad screamed back.

"Who are you talking to, *boy*?" the man asked.

"There's only two of us talking, so you figure it out," my dad said cooly. "And there ain't nothing but the wind between us, so you can come back here and talk to me like that to my face."

Well, he did.

That foolish man was emboldened by the belief that the color of his skin meant he could get away with anything. He stalked toward and slapped my dad, who was holding two arms of tobacco. My dad threw the tobacco in that man's face, tackled him, and put a beating on him until the Black coworkers pulled him off.

Those coworkers then ran from the field as fast as they could and yelled back that my dad had better do the same, but faster and further.

My dad sprinted all the way home and had to admit that his mother was right. He and trouble had found one another yet again.

But his parents had no desire to gloat. They were worried for his safety, so they quickly packed my dad's belongings and drove him to Forest, Mississippi, to stay with his father's sister. She was a schoolteacher whom the family affectionately called "Sergeant" because she was known to straighten out kids.

It turned out to be a blessing. My dad was a star athlete back in Perry, both in basketball and football, to the point that he had numerous college scholarships at the end of his junior year of high school. There was concern that the move would cost him the opportunity to go to college.

But in Mississippi, during his senior year, he was again the big man on campus, both literally and figuratively, adding more scholarship offers from different colleges that might not have seen him play in Florida.

He initially said no to all of them.

Why go to college and put off earning a full-time income for four years, he figured, when he could work immediately? That infuriated his father.

It was safe to return to Perry by then, so my dad moved back into his parents' home with the thought that he would work while living rent and bill free so he could stash away some money.

His father had other plans. My dad was ordered to pay his mother $20 a week to stay there.

"But that would be half of what I could earn in a week," he pled. "What am I paying my mama for?"

"For washing, ironing, cooking, and a place to stay," his dad explained with a smile. He knew exactly what he was doing.

"I never had to pay mama for that before," my dad argued.

"Well, you've never been grown before," his father shot back.

My dad was furious and determined to get as far away from his dad as possible. So he called his basketball coach from his junior year in Perry and asked if any of those scholarships were still available.

Absolutely, the coach told him. There were standing offers from schools in Alabama, South Carolina, and Georgia.

Those were not good enough for my dad. The schools were fine, and their teams were excellent, but he would still be too close to his dad.

So he called his basketball coach from Mississippi and asked the same question.

One scholarship offer in particular stood out to my dad: Paul Quinn College. It was in Waco, Texas, and as far from Perry as he could get.

So he took the scholarship, and for three years he ruled the court. There was even talk that he would go to the NBA. But near the end of my dad's junior season, he suffered a knee injury and was told he would never be the same player again.

The university pulled his scholarship, but he was too close to that diploma to give up. So he transferred to Florida A&M University, which was close enough to his parents' house to commute, found a part-time job, and paid his way through graduation.

I asked my dad once if he harbored any anger over losing the opportunity to play professional basketball.

Absolutely not, he explained. He was such a glass half-full type of guy.

Instead, he had nothing but positive memories of collegiate sports. Without them, he would likely have never gone to college. His scholarship gave him three paid years of college. And that education enabled him to become a transformational figure who could prevent scenes like what played out on that farm years earlier.

Sports, he said, are not only about dreams of playing professionally. Sports are about the opportunities that they create for you off the court and field. And those opportunities are not just scholarships. Most will not get a scholarship. The best opportunity that sports present is the opportunity to grow as a person.

It doesn't matter if you win, lose, or draw, are MVP or LVP, he always preached to me. "I will criticize you if you win and don't put forth your best effort," my dad would say, "but I will compliment you if you lose but play your hardest."

He worked to instill that in me and any young man he came across. Give it your best effort, your best shot, and be satisfied with that. Whether you win or lose, congratulate your opponent at the end of the game. Learn how to win and learn how to lose: don't showboat when you win, or curse, get down on yourself, or make excuses when you lose. Build character, learn how to be part of a team, and forge relationships. And apply all of those skills to your personal and professional life. Those will help you to become a better and more successful man.

Sports, he used to say, can be a window to someone's soul and show us what needs improvement.

If someone is lazy at sports practice, they will likely be lazy at their job. But if they work hard at practice, they will likely work hard at their job.

If someone complains that the drills are too hard, they will likely complain that their workload at the office is too much. If someone puts their head down and competes in every drill without a whimper, they will likely bring that same attitude to the office.

If someone is a bad leader in a game, they will likely be a bad boss. But if someone is a great leader in a game, they will likely be a great boss.

None of those positive attributes require someone to be the star of the team or even decent at the sport.

Sports, my father would say, offer us an opportunity to work on those deficiencies and improve ourselves.

Sports can be utilized to build a lot of things: work ethic, mental strength, character, and leadership abilities. We all must become professional at something, and it likely will not be sports. But these characteristics that are learned through sports can be transferred to any skill set in any profession.

For many of us, sports, and all competition, give us an outlet. But they also give us an opportunity to become a great teammate, a great leader, a great mother, a great father, a great son, or a great daughter by providing us opportunities to engage with other people from the same and different backgrounds.

Maybe you are one of the few parents whose child will become a professional athlete. But most likely, they will not. Please put childhood sports in perspective.

Let your kids have fun and use sports to help them grow. There was nothing about my earliest days on the football field that had anyone thinking I would one day be a Division I football player for the greatest collegiate sports program in the nation— the University of Florida—and one day become a professional athlete, first with a brief stint for the Jacksonville Jaguars before a knee injury, then with the Arena Football League, and then for WWE, a world that I never considered a possibility.

When I was playing football at 10 years old, I was surrounded by great athletes, and I was the odd man out. I was tall, skinny, and wore such thick glasses that my teammates and coaches nicknamed me "Eyes." I did not get into a game until week six. I recorded a tackle, but it was more of a "sort of tackle." The running back tripped on his own. I just jumped on to take the statistic—tackle for a loss. But my coaches and teammates celebrated like we had won the Super Bowl. Looking back, I now understand why. Sometimes, the person who you think will not do anything outworks everybody, is very respectful to the game, and treats their teammates well. You end up rooting for that guy or that girl. I was that person, and that's a great person to be. But that person doesn't typically go on to become a professional athlete.

No, no one would have thought that I would one day earn a living through my athletic ability.

But I'm sure many expected that my sons would be great athletes before they even picked up a ball or could walk, simply because of their DNA.

While I had humble athletic beginnings, I clearly excelled in my teen years. I was a *USA Today* and *Parade* magazine high school All-American as a defensive end, and a top recruit for the University of Florida, where I totaled 56 tackles, nine of which were for a loss, plus two sacks.

My sons' mother was also a student athlete as a softball player and track runner. You might also know her brother and my former collegiate teammate, Earnest Graham, who is not only an athletic legend in Lee County but also a Gator Great and Florida-Georgia Hall of Famer. Here are a few of his athletic highlights: He rushed for nearly 6,000 yards and 86 touchdowns in high school, and at the conclusion of his collegiate career, ranked third in the university's running back history with 33 touchdowns, fifth in both rushing yards — with 3,065, and 100-yard games, with nine — and ninth in all-purpose yards. He was then signed as an undrafted free agent by my hometown Buccaneers, for whom he amassed 2,047 rushing yards and 15 touchdowns over eight seasons.

My kids' mother's other two brothers were also both stud athletes.

With such genetics coming from both sides of their family tree, others likely expected great things from my children.

I did not expect a thing. What they did with their bodies never mattered to me.

Sure, I had hoped that they enjoyed playing and watching sports. What father doesn't want his children to have similar interests? What father doesn't dream of one day throwing a football or baseball with their kids? When it comes to youth sports, I don't think the quality time they provide gets as much credit as it deserves.

Even as a father who has been involved in sports for his entire life, I did not want to put any pressure on them, in the same way that a family of artists or doctors should not expect their kids to become artists or doctors too. I was aware that putting such pressure on children to "be like me" can sometimes completely turn them away from following a certain path or cause them to harbor anger with a parent because they were never interested in that activity.

And I knew that while athletic genetics are passed down, that doesn't ensure anything. After all, Michael Jordan and Magic Johnson were the two best basketball players of my youth, yet neither had kids who went pro. I'm sure that both Magic and Michael would do everything and provide every resource possible if sports were a venture that their children wanted to explore. But sometimes the cards don't come up as we hope. Sometimes a child doesn't desire to follow in the footsteps of their hero father or mother. Sometimes, even if they do, no matter how hard they work, they cannot match the parent's achievements, and putting too much pressure on them to do so could have a negative impact on their lives.

My focus was never on developing my sons into great and professional athletes. I wanted to develop them into great and professional human beings. I wanted to develop the mindset that regardless of the extracurricular activity, whether it was sports, arts, or music, that they should utilize those venues and arenas to help them become greater overall human beings.

It did not take long for me to realize that both of my sons were athletically skilled.

When they first began to walk, the first sport they participated in was soccer. Like many kids at a young age, that came with a lot of falls and tumbles. Insert *Royal Rumble* moment here.

I support all coaches who volunteer to oversee a team. But I especially salute those who coach the real little ones.

At that age, it's less like a sport and more like herding cats.

Every single one of those soccer teams seems to have the same cast of characters. There is the kid who twirls in circles for the entirety of the game, the kid who refuses to play, the kid who picks their nose and the grass, and the kid who pretends to shoot Spiderman webs at others.

And then each team has one kid, or two on some occasions, who seem to get it.

While the rest of the players just kick the ball as far as they can—maybe a few inches—when it happens to roll to them, one kid per team just seems to naturally understand the purpose of the game. They dribble the ball down field and kick it into the net time and time again. If the final score is 10–9, those outliers can account for 17 of the goals, with the other two coming when the ball happens to bounce off another player and roll into the net.

My sons were those kids who excelled in those early soccer seasons, and later excelled at each new sport they tried.

I began taking TJ and Titus to the golf course regularly when they were five and three years old, respectively. They picked up that complicated game quickly, much quicker than I did. Friends would exclaim that I had two Tiger Woods on my hands, and this was when Tiger might have been the most popular athlete in the world, maybe even more so than MJ himself. Sure, there were voices inside my head telling me to push them into golf and turn them into stars. Again, I'm human. But I also knew that was the wrong approach. I did not want them to feel that pressure or grow up believing that their lives were controlled by athletics. It wasn't up to me to choose that direction for them. Only they could make that decision, and only when they got older. If the wait cost them precious years of training and set them back, so be it.

For me, introducing them to the game of golf was more about putting them in a situation that's familiar to me: on a golf course, conducting business and networking. Heck, I have even played in a few LIV Golf pro-ams. At my first, my team beat Phil Mickelson's team by one point to win the entire tournament. I also hit closest to the pin to secure our entire team a custom-made putter from LA Golf. Not bad for my first pro-am.

I wanted the game of golf to be something that was relaxing to my kids, something that they enjoy, something that, when they get older, they can take up more seriously and play during their retirement years. They could also use it to play at charity and celebrity golf tournaments while in college. But as for whether they made golf their go-to number one sport—that had to be entirely up to them.

As my kids grew older, I continued to realize that sports are a great tool to mold them.

When it became apparent that neither would be challenged by playing against kids who were their own age, I moved them up to compete against older children. I did not want them to grow up dominating the competition. I wanted to see how they would react when pushed and when they were the underdog. I wanted to see if they were willing to rise to the challenge.

When it comes to sports, I'm somewhat of a perfectionist but always a professional. But with my kids, my emphasis was less about being a perfectionist and more about being professional. I would never force either of my sons to have anything remotely close to my competitive personality, but they both do.

Not only would they want to play football on off days, but they also regularly requested that I work with them before and after practices. We would arrive early to the field and often stay late to work on things like footwork, hand placement, and other drills that could make them better and more complete players. On some nights, we would sit and watch game film to discuss what they were doing right or wrong or to scout the opposing team of the upcoming game. I would weigh in with constructive advice, but I must stress it was their decision to work that hard.

I did not break out as an athlete until I was a junior in high school. My oldest, TJ, had his breakout much earlier.

He was 11 or 12 and had a monster performance as wide receiver and outside linebacker in his youth football team's semifinal game. He had three or four really big plays on defense, including a forced fumble and a recovered fumble, plus two touchdowns on amazing catches on offense.

After that performance, TJ's coach compared him to a young Kelvin Benjamin, a wide receiver who had been a first-round pick by the Carolina Panthers.

It was flattering, but I did not completely indulge in that comparison. After all, Kelvin had played for the enemy, Florida State University.

But seriously, while I was proud of how he played that day, looking back, I'm prouder of one of his failures.

He missed two key free throws in the final minute of an important AAU basketball tournament game. The team won, but TJ still felt that he let them down. Just 10 at the time, TJ woke up early the next day and asked for a ride to the local court so that he could practice free throws. Standing in the Florida heat, he must have stood at that line for three hours as I rebounded for him.

It was at that moment that I knew for a fact that TJ would be more than okay in life.

Titus had similar moments.

When Titus was around 13, he got into a confrontation with an opposing player during a football game. As the coach was speaking to him, Titus lashed out in response. I lost my cool. As a parent, I try my best to make sure that my children always respect adults, especially the adults who are responsible for making sure that they become the best that they can be. Titus's actions did not sit well with me at all. I pulled him to the side and had a not-so-pleasant conversation with him. I instructed the coaches that he would not be returning to the game and told Titus there was a chance that might have been his last football game of the season.

While this wasn't an athletic failure, it was a failure on an athletic field that we utilized as a teachable moment. He admitted he was out of line and promised to never do anything like that again. I told him I was proud that he owned up to it.

I don't know if either will play professional football.

Maybe they will—though the odds are surely against them. Less than 2 percent of those who play a collegiate sport make it to the pros. But one thing I do know for sure is that they will be great professionals in whatever they decide to do in life.

The lessons they learned and continue to learn while playing sports will carry them very far.

———

Here are some media excerpts announcing my oldest son's decision to play football for the University of Central Florida:

> "Berkeley Prep linebacker TJ Bullard announced he will play for UCF football Saturday night on Twitter. Bullard is the son of Thaddeus Bullard, who wrestles under the name Titus O'Neil in WWE. Thaddeus is a former defensive end for the Florida State Gators, playing from 1997 till 2000." —WFLA

> "Berkeley Prep linebacker TJ Bullard has orally committed to UCF, he announced on Saturday night. Bullard is the son of Thaddeus Bullard, the former Gators defensive end (1997–2000) who's a pro wrestling Superstar under the name Titus O'Neil." —*Tampa Bay Times*

> "UCF Nights football has added some star power to its fan base with the commitment of linebacker

TJ Bullard. Bullard, the son of WWE Superstar Titus O'Neil, announced his commitment to UCF on Saturday."—blackandgoldbanneret.com

"High above the craziness of downtown Orlando's Orange Avenue on Saturday night, TJ Bullard was having his own celebration this past weekend. Accompanied by the entire UCF coaching staff, which treated Bullard, his parents, and a few other visitors to the ambiance and 18th-floor views from the Citrus Club, Bullard decided it was time to let UCF coaches know of his intentions to commit to the Knights football program. Bullard, the son of Thaddeus Bullard, a former Florida defensive end and short-time NFL player who became WWE star Titus O'Neil after his football career, told the group Saturday night he would be a Knight."
—*Orlando Sentinel*

My name was included in every other article too.

I'm certain that he did not have a problem with that. I know that he is proud of me. He is proud that I'm his father, but I have never tried to outshine my children in any way, shape, or form.

I'm a big guy.

I stand at six-foot-four and usually walk around at 270 pounds.

As a professional athlete and global Superstar, I can occasionally cast a larger shadow, one that can sometimes eclipse my sons' special moments.

Being the child of a professional athlete has its advantages. Yes, I have skills and knowledge that I can pass on. But more importantly, I have relationships with coaches and athletic friends who can step in to help my sons with things that I cannot.

But being the child of a professional athlete also has its drawbacks. Sometimes the shadow *is* overshadowing.

Sometimes, that shadow can bring in fans. People who rooted for the parent may root for their children.

In WWE, there are numerous second and third generation Superstars. And while, yes, those Superstars grew beyond the shadows of their family members, they also had to work hard to establish themselves as legitimate and formidable Superstars. While the platform and the fan base of WWE can be amazing for some, it can be brutal for others, especially second and third generation Superstars because the WWE Universe wants to ensure nobody is just handed an opportunity.

For example, look no further than Dwayne "The Rock" Johnson who, despite being booked as a good guy upon his initial run in WWE, was booed unmercifully. It wasn't until The Rock stepped away from his father's shadow and found his own voice that he became one of the biggest pop culture sensations in the world. The same could be said for my friends Cody Rhodes and Charlotte Flair. Both of their famous fathers were part of their early pushes but stepped aside to let the spotlight shine on their kids.

It's even something my friend Mark Henry would say his children have had to overcome in their youth athletics.

The word *overcome* might seem like an exaggeration.

After all, as Mark points out, there are a lot of advantages to being the children of the World's Strongest Man and a WWE Hall of Famer. His connections and success allows for them to receive the best of the best, the best private coaches and the best private trainers who help them get into the best shape and have the best technique.

Mark doesn't do that to spoil them. He does it because he loves them; because he wants them to succeed; because, most importantly, they want to succeed. He knows his children will be judged more than any other athlete in a competition because they have a famous father who is former Olympian, professional athlete, and WWE legend.

His son, Jacob, has a larger shadow cast on him because of his weightlifting ability. In 2023, as a 17-year-old junior in high school, Jacob was squatting 650 pounds, deadlifting 600 pounds, and benching 375 pounds as a six-foot-one, 280-pound defensive lineman and heavyweight high school wrestler.

Jacob has publicly lamented that people attribute his success to his father, as though DNA is the only reason he is a stellar athlete. Genetics helps, but Jacob succeeds because he puts in the work.

Other wrestlers often target Jacob on their schedule so they can brag that they beat the son of the great Mark Henry. Then, of course, they lay eyes on Jacob for the first time and wonder if they are in over their heads. And then they feel his strength on the mat and realize that, yes, they are in over their heads. And that is why, despite the shadow of the World's Strongest Man, Jacob has been able to make a mark of his own.

My shadow is also why, while I was an active father and one who rarely missed a game, I did my best to ensure that the spotlight was on my kids. I never wanted the moment to be about me.

I coached my sons when they were little, but as they got older, my celebrity grew and so did my travel schedule and calendar of responsibilities. That relegated me to fan only, and that might have been a good thing. At games, rather than being the parent who sat front and center in the stands and cheered the loudest, I'd prefer to stand in a corner of the court or field and simply watch, away from the eyes of others so that those eyes remained on the players. And before the first practice, I'd approach my kids' coaches to introduce myself and assure them that I was there only as a fan and I would not overstep my boundaries or step on their toes. I'd also make sure they knew to reach out to me if my sons were ever disrespectful or not working hard. I wanted it to be clear that the sport was about my kids and the team and not about me, at all. I'm neither on the team as player nor coach. I'm simply a spectator and a supporter, and that is where my role has stayed during their entire sports careers.

I always remind my sons that the only expectation that they need to meet is how they act. No fussing. No complaining. No poor sportsmanship. I can't stop people from wanting to compare them to me or other members of our family, but that doesn't mean they have to pay any attention to such people. Be your own person, I tell them, and people will see you as your own person.

I like to believe that my approach was successful. Yes, my name was mentioned by the media covering TJ's college signing, but he was still the lede and headline. I was secondary. He shared his moment with me, but it was still his moment.

This is not just a lesson for celebrity parents. This is a lesson for all parents.

Anyone can steal their child's thunder if they are not careful. I see too many parents who make their kids' sports all about them at games, practices, and back at home.

For those who are sports parents, ask yourselves, "Am I that parent?"

Here are the types of bad sports parents who make the sport too much about them.

Sideline referee: Stop yelling at the referees, judges, and umpires. Stop blaming them for a loss or your child's poor performance. Most of those men and women, who are sometimes teenagers, are performing that job for the love of the game and are earning peanuts. They don't deserve your abuse. An athletic competition is decided by numerous factors, not just a few calls that you perceive as bad. When you are that parent who is foaming at the mouth on the sideline, suddenly you become the main attraction and your child becomes an afterthought. A child can go 4-for-4 with four home runs in a baseball game, but I guarantee others at the game will remember that star's parent for cursing at the referee or, worse, getting into an altercation over anything the child accomplished.

Sideline coach: I'm all for coaching your child at home. And I completely understand that we don't all have time to volunteer as team coaches, so I will not give the "If you don't like what you see, volunteer" lecture. Work, family commitments, and other obligations prevent many from volunteering. But don't overdo it when yelling instructions at your child from the sideline, even if you believe that the advice is sound. Don't be that parent who yells instructions throughout the duration of an athletic competition. In fact, try not to yell any instructions at all. Maybe what you're telling your child is not what the coach wants. Maybe your child understands what you want but doesn't have the ability to do it yet. Maybe you are putting too much pressure on your child by coaching from the sideline. By sideline coaching too aggressively, you might take the focus off your child and put it on yourself. People in the stands will be staring at you, the obnoxious parent, and not your child.

Bully cheerleader: I cannot control what you think. If inside your brain, you choose to wish athletic failure upon other young children so that your child succeeds, that's all on you. But doing so vocally makes you a bully. You are bullying other kids. And that includes putting other kids down under the guise of advice. I have heard parents yell to their child pitchers, "Just put the ball over the plate; this kid can't hit." Or, "Foul the kid. He can't shoot free throws" during a basketball game. I don't like it when fans disrespect professional players. When I hear parents disrespect kids, especially little ones, my blood boils. And don't tell me you are acting out of love because you want your kid to succeed. Those parents act like that because they want the moment to be about them. Such parents are usually overly competitive because they care more about bragging about their kid's athletic success than setting a good example. The game is about kids. It's not about you. Those parents typically come from the same mold. They never lived up to their own athletic expectations, so they now place that burden on their children.

The overly excited parents of kids who are not excited to be there: Not every kid will love sports. Many children would prefer to stay home to read, play chess, paint pictures, or practice a musical instrument. I understand if you want your child to play a sport because you feel it's important they get exercise and learn the lessons that come with athletics. But if sports are not important to your kids, don't let sports be more important to you. Match your level with their level so they don't feel too much pressure, which can ruin their fun. Again, it's about the kid, not you.

The winning-is-everything parent: Some parents are obvious about it. Others are more subtle, treating their child differently after a well-played individual performance or victory than a poor individual performance or loss. That sets the tone that your love is contingent on athletic excellence. And not to sound like a broken record, but there is no other reason for acting like that other than your need to fill a childhood void.

———

Mark Henry was recently hit with an interesting dilemma.

His daughter, Joanna, is one of the most naturally gifted athletes you can meet. Mark says that you could tell from the moment she could crawl that she was destined to dominate whatever sport she chose. But which would she choose?

When his kids were little, Mark allowed both to try every sport they could imagine. It had to be up to them. They tried it all: lacrosse, soccer, volleyball, basketball, softball, martial arts, weightlifting. If they decided to pursue one more seriously than the other, Mark promised that he would provide them with the opportunities to succeed, but they had to be willing to work. Don't waste his money and time, he would tell them. And if they lost interest in the sport and no longer wanted to compete in it, he would not pressure them to keep it up, no matter how much time and money he had already put into it. It's their life to live. He is just there to support them.

But words can be easy to say. What happens you have to live up to them?

Mark was faced with that when, after competing in multiple Junior Olympics for sprints and throwing, Joanna decided to give up track and field. She seemed destined for a college scholarship, yet lost interest and preferred to focus on wrestling and volleyball. Mark admitted he initially wondered if he needed to talk sense into her, but she was adamant that the sport was no longer for her. So without knowing if she could rise to the same level in the other sports, he agreed that she had to follow her heart. She is killing it in wrestling and volleyball, but hindsight is 20/20. There was no guarantee. But the way Mark saw it, even if she wasn't as good, so what? The most important thing is that she is happy and that she is doing what *she* wants to do.

Joanna's life is not about Mark. It's about Joanna.

Let's take a quiz.

I'm going to detail three stories of child athletes who my friend Ricky Sailor's Unsigned Preps have helped. I then want you to tell me which one is the greatest success story of the three.

Nelson Vazquez was a standout wide receiver at Tampa's Plant High School, where he led the team to a 14–1 record and a state title in 2008. Unsigned Preps then helped Vazquez sign with Mendocino College, a community college in Ukiah, California, where he enjoyed great success with 32 catches, 517 yards, and eight touchdowns as a sophomore, which helped him to next move on to Fort Hays State University, a Division II school in Hays, Kansas. There, injuries limited his playing time and on-field success. He next went into coaching, first as a wide receivers coach at his high school alma mater, Plant High, then Wesley Chapel High School, and then onto college at New Mexico Military State Institute, where he was later promoted to passing game coordinator and quarterbacks coach, with more promotions surely to come.

Kobie Jones starred as a quarterback at Dunnellon High School before Unsigned Preps helped him sign with Alabama State, where, after redshirting his freshman year, he entered the 2017 season starting behind center. He had a good season. Splitting time with another quarterback, he accumulated 575 yards on 72-for-129 passing and three touchdowns against five interceptions while also scrambling for 136 yards on 45 carries. But the following season, it was decided that he would move to defensive back. He did not see any action that season and played in four games the following season. He went on to work as a defensive ends coach for IMG Academy before accepting a defensive graduate position for the University of Alabama.

Tyree St. Louis was an offensive tackle for IMG Academy and then, with the help of Unsigned Preps, moved on to play the same position for the University of Miami, where he made an immediate impact on special teams during his freshman season. He earned a starting offensive lineman position during his sophomore season and never relinquished it. In 2018, he was honorable mention All-ACC and then signed with the New England Patriots as an undrafted free agent but spent the season as part of the Los Angeles Chargers practice squad. The following season, he earned a spot on the Los Angeles Chargers roster and debuted in their opening game. He was injured and released the following season. He then signed with the United States Football League's Birmingham Stallions, where he played until announcing his retirement in March 2023.

So who do you believe is the greatest success of the three?

If you said Tyree St. Louis because he made it to the NFL, then you need to take stock of your priorities.

Oh, you should be proud of him. He set a goal to make it to the NFL and succeeded.

But the correct answer is that all three are equal successes. Each graduated from high school and then college and have forged careers in a field they love. They should all be proud of what they accomplished. One being a professional athlete doesn't make him more successful.

In fact, my proudest moment for Tyree has nothing to do with his on-field play.

While at the University of Miami, Tyree continued the community service work that he learned to do through Unsigned Preps. During one of his collegiate years, Unsigned Preps awarded him the Tyrone Keys Community Service Award. But he was faced with a transportation issue and had no way to get to the event. He could have canceled his appearance and had someone accept in his honor. Instead, Tyree, a collegiate standout and future NFL player, got on a bus and took the long uncomfortable journey to Tampa. He could not disappoint the kids who would be in that audience; he wanted to show them that they too could go to college if they put their minds to it.

That is the definition of success.

———

Over the course of his first 34 seasons as a high school football head coach in Hillsborough County—17 with Jesuit High School and then another 17 with Berkeley Preparatory School—Dominick Ciao amassed 265 victories, but many will wrongly judge his career by one win: his first state title in 2023.

My son Titus was on that team and played an oversized role in the title victory by accumulating two and half sacks, one of which included a forced fumble that led to a turnover and offensive touchdown. As his father, I beamed with pride as I witnessed my son's years of hard work pay off on such a grand stage.

The Bullards are a family of winners.

During all of my years as a football player, from peewee through high school, college, and then the pros, I never once competed on a team with a losing record and accumulated titles along the way. My two sons, TJ and Titus, can say the same to this point in their lives, as can my daughter, Leah, who, as a member of her high school's varsity basketball team since the seventh grade, has played in five state title games, won two, and will hopefully celebrate a sixth as a senior before this book comes out.

To reiterate, victories alone do not make you a winner.

Even before he won a state championship, Coach Ciao was the ultimate winner in my opinion. He never had children of his own but was a mentor to hundreds. Around 150 of his players went on to college football careers and countless others got into college by adapting the skills they learned on the field to achieve excellence in the classroom.

In 2016, Coach Ciao was recognized by the Positive Coaching Alliance with its Double-Goal Coach Award, which is presented to coaches who strive to win while pursuing the more important goal of teaching life lessons through sports.

While I understand that Coach Ciao would likely place the state title trophy in the most prominent place in a trophy case, I know that he also views the Double-Goal award as a career highlight. He might only have one state title as of the end of the 2023 season, but he finishes every season a champion for the way he mentors young men into adults.

———

The year 2021 was a launch party of sorts for the University of Central Florida's football program, which had been on a steady rise for the last half decade.

In 2021, UCF accepted a bid to play in the Union Home Mortgage Gasparilla Bowl in my home city of Tampa, marking their six consecutive postseason appearance, ninth in 10 seasons and 13th in 17 years.

But that Gasparilla Bowl was different. They were facing my University of Florida, a historic program that I believed would again steamroll UCF as they had in their two previous meetings: 42–0 in 2006 and 59–27 in 1999.

It did not go Florida's way that year.

As the *Tampa Bay Times* put it, UCF beat UF in every phase of the game en route to a 29–17 victory that wasn't as close as the score.

The Knights won the offensive battle with 436 yards to the Gators' 376.

The Knights won the defensive battle by forcing three three-and-outs in the second half, stopping 11 of 13 third-down conversions, and taking the air out of the ball by holding Florida QB Emory Jones to just 171 yards in a season in which he put up more than 2,700 yards.

They won on special teams in a game that saw Florida miss two field goals to UCF's one miss.

And the best player on the field was a Knight. Ryan O'Keefe finished with 251 all-purpose yards—100 rushing, 85 receiving, and 56 on-kick returns.

As the Knights coach Gus Malzhan repeated in the post-game press conference, "We beat them handily." Which they did.

But what I will forever remember most about that game is that it was the first time my house was a house divided. I, of course, rooted for Florida. But my son TJ, who had rooted alongside me since he was in diapers, was a UCF fan that day, and for an obvious reason: just a few months earlier, he had committed to the Knights for the following school year.

And that was fine with me. I grew up a diehard Florida State University fan. I bled the garnet and gold primarily due to Charlie Ward, the most exciting quarterback of my formative years. So when it became apparent that I had high-level Division I football talent, most expected me to go to Florida State.

I expected to go there too. I went on a recruiting trip and met with their players and the legendary Bobby Bowden. Everything about the university lived up to my expectations.

But the University of Florida exceeded my expectations as well.

It wasn't an easy decision.

There was a lot of pressure placed on me to pick the Florida State Seminoles.

My mother's father, whom I had never met prior to that recruiting phase, appeared out of nowhere to become a part of my life and pressure me to go to Florida State.

My high school's stars typically chose to become Seminoles, so coaches, teachers, and fans let me know that they expected me to do the same.

But my dad, Mr. Blalock, refused to allow anyone to pressure me into making a decision. In fact, he was the opposite. When I pondered going to his alma mater, Florida A&M University, a decision for which he could have taken credit and been applauded, he talked me out of it. He would be proud to see me follow in his footsteps, my dad said, but my feet were meant for larger shoes than FAMU could provide. He repeatedly told me I was the one who would have to go to practice and class for four years. He refused to let me allow outside influences impact my decision.

So when it came time for TJ's recruitment, I repeated the same advice to him over and over again. There were some who wondered if I would be all talk when rubber hit the road.

It was one thing to tell my son that I would be okay if he chose to play football for a college other than Florida University. But would I change my tune if the opportunity arose?

Early on, it did not seem like I had anything to worry about. Florida University did not recruit him.

TJ's finalists were the University of Louisville, University of Central Florida, Cincinnati, and Yale. Yale was the early front-runner, but they don't offer full scholarships. He ultimately fell in love with UCF and said that was the easy choice.

Then, as signing day approached, Florida University and Florida State University popped up and showed interest.

His cousin, Myles Graham, had already accepted an offer as a linebacker for the Gators.

TJ was also being recruited as a linebacker. Part of me thought that it would be great to see my son and nephew playing side by side at my alma mater.

But I kept my mouth shut.

It. Was. Not. My. Decision.

It. Was. Not. My. Life.

And it wasn't a hard decision for TJ. He never wavered—it was UCF all the way.

I do wonder what I'll do when Florida University and UCF square off again when my son is part of the game. Actually, I don't wonder. I will root for my son to have the greatest game possible. But, deep down, I'll want the Gators to come out on top.

But it doesn't really matter who I cheer for.

The game will not be about me.

It will be about my son.

CHAPTER 10

WHEN THE NEST EMPTIES

A s a kid, there were lots of resources I could not readily access. Eyeglasses were one.

At the time, I was too embarrassed to let my teachers know that I could not see and was definitely embarrassed that we could not afford to get the glasses that I needed. So I pretended like all was well, even sitting in the back of the class to perpetuate that my vision was 20/20 and so that I could avoid being called upon.

In around third or fourth grade, a social worker helped me get a pair of glasses, but I was again too embarrassed to wear them when tape was needed to hold them together after a fight with a bully.

That meant I spent most of my early childhood unprepared for tests, so I often did poorly.

The first time I stayed away from home was during the summer before eighth grade. My mother sent me to a week-long camp meant to assist young men who were getting into trouble. It was set deep in the woods and was beautifully scenic and fun. Activities included canoeing, archery, and campfires. At night, far from any light pollution, we could see every star visible to the human eye.

But my first day there was neither beautiful nor fun. I was constantly worried that a snake would slither into my tent or that I would get attacked by a wild boar, bear, or lion.

I'm grateful to say that nothing bad happened to me. All of my wildest fears dissipated when I realized, after speaking with the camp counselors, that there was no way I was going to be eaten by a lion or bitten by a snake.

In retrospect, I realize the counselors never did mention that I was safe from boars . . .

Also in retrospect, I realize that I was afraid because it was my first time away from home and my first time camping. I wasn't prepared.

Early on, I struggled to adapt to life at the Florida Sheriffs Boys Ranch in Live Oak, a program meant to rehabilitate young men and women, where my mother and I agreed that I should move to straighten out my life. I struggled to accept that Live Oak was my new hometown. To be blunt, it was white . . . very white. I was more than a minority there. I was a rarity. There were maybe a few handfuls of Black families living in the town off the ranch. So once I left the ranch, I stood out like a sore thumb.

And then there were my "cottage parents," as they were called—a husband and wife who lived with us in our dormitory-styled cottage. We were expected to call them Mom and Pop, but I had an issue with that. They were white and I was Black, and there was no way that I was going to pretend that anyone who was white was my parent.

One of my many issues was that I had very little experience interacting with white people, especially white people in positions of authority, other than the negative interactions with teachers. And due to that lack of positive diverse interactions, I was unprepared for the experience.

The first time one of my sons ever went away for any extended period of time was when 13-year-old TJ joined one of Unsigned Prep's week-long bus trips. It took elite student athletes to different college campuses to tour the facilities, meet the coaches and recruiters, and compete against other athletes. It was meant to help get them started in the recruitment process, bond with others who have the same or better skill level, and, for some, make the dream of attending college look like a real possibility.

TJ's trip took him to the University of Florida, Florida State University, the University of Georgia, and the University of Alabama. You already know my favorite spot: the University of Florida.

I thought that I was ready to see him leave the nest for a week.

I knew each destination he was going to. I knew the coaches and chaperone. I knew he would be well taken care of throughout the trip. I had been on the road since he was born, so I was accustomed to being separated from him. Plus, even when I was in Tampa, he was sometimes at his mother's house.

Yet I was uncomfortable. I wasn't prepared. It was the first extended period of time that neither his mother nor I were with him.

It was the first time that I had no way to know what or how he was doing.

I would not say I was worried. I knew he was in great hands and would survive and even thrive. But I wondered, constantly. I wondered how he was approaching and bonding with others. I wondered what feedback he was getting. I wondered if he was eating healthy and stretching properly. I wondered how he was sleeping. I wondered, and I wondered, and I wondered.

I found myself, throughout that week, wondering if it was alright for me to check in on him. I did a few times, but not as often as I wanted. I knew that I had to give him space to grow as a man without me. I wondered how often I could check on him without crossing the line.

I wondered what was wrong with me. Why was I wondering so much?

If I was experiencing this amount of wonderment when he was gone for just a week, how would I react when he was out of the house for good?

I wondered if I would ever be prepared for that day.

It turned out that I was fine when that day came, but not because I was prepared.

For most of my adulthood, I was against owning a dog. I figured that I spent too much time on the road to handle such a responsibility.

But as my sons got older and promised that they could handle the dog while I was traveling, I finally gave in.

We took home our first French bulldog during TJ's senior and Titus's junior year. He is happily named Ali, after one of the all-time great humanitarians who also happened to be one of the greatest boxers of all-time: Muhammad Ali.

Not long after Ali joined our family, a friend from New York called to ask if I knew of anyone looking for a French bulldog. She had recently adopted one named Saint but quickly realized that she could not give him the attention he needed. Of course I knew someone, I told her: me. So, like that, I was a dog dad to two French bulldogs.

Bringing Saint to my household was much harder than it had been for Ali. I purchased Ali from a local breeder here in Tampa. And once TJ confirmed that Ali was the dog we should get, it was a wrap. I paid my money, filled out the paperwork, and Ali joined our family.

Saint was the complete opposite. I had not met Saint before getting him. I saw a picture, but that was it. I asked a different friend in New York to fly him down to me, but that idea was nixed because Saint is not a service dog and was too big to fly as a passenger dog. So the friend offered to drive Saint to my family. Yes, from New York. My friend is a saint too.

When Saint first arrived, he was trembling. Apparently, he had thrown up the majority of his food on the ride down. I did not judge. I probably would have too. That is a long ride to not get carsick. Plus, I'm sure he was homesick.

I immediately fell in love with Saint, but he did need training. So I sent him to my niece and nephew, so that their Canine Cardio dog training business could properly train him to be the ultimate member of the family. They were successful.

I later helped friends get Stitch, also a French bulldog, but that did not work out for them, so I ended up with him too.

And once I had three, I figured how much harder could a fourth French bulldog be? Upon our meeting, I immediately fell in love with another, whom I named Frazier after another great humanitarian who happened to have one of the greatest left hooks in the history of boxing. And luckily my Ali doesn't taunt my Frazier.

They are each unique. Ali thinks he is the parent because he was first. Frazier will not let any of the others become bullies. Saint, while saintly, is not a saint, at all, and while none are misbehaved, he is the closest. And Stitch just kind of marches to his own drum. He doesn't need to be with the others and is happy playing by himself outside all day.

I recall as TJ was getting closer to going off to college, a friend remarked that having four dogs would make it easier for me.

I love my dogs, but that was a silly statement.

My dogs can't go to concerts or sporting events with me. They can go to the gym with me, but they'd make terrible spotters. My dogs can join me out for dinner at only a few restaurants that allow them on their patio. And while they can sit on the couch with me and watch television, my dogs are terrible conversationalists. Nothing can replace my kids.

Not all the dogs in the world, plus the cats, hamsters, rabbits, and giraffes.

And not to offend anyone who is a cat person: I absolutely despise cats. I have feared cats since I was a kid, when I saw them scratch people. I have never trusted them.

I'm more likely to be a proud owner of a pet giraffe than a cat.

———

I was shocked that neither TJ nor I were overly emotional when I took him to college for the start of preseason football workouts. We drove to Orlando the night before he was to check in, stayed at a hotel, woke early the next morning, drove to campus, shared a short embrace, I reminded him that I was proud as hell and that I knew he was going to kill it, and then said our goodbyes with a hug and handshake. Not a voice cracked. Not a tear was shed, at least, not at that moment. I have never asked TJ if he was emotional and cried the day that I dropped him off. I'm sure he would tell me the truth. But then again, he might be too embarrassed to share.

Initially, I thought that my lack of emotion was because I knew I would see him again very soon.

I returned the following weekend to help TJ deck out his dorm room with a new bed, dressers, lamps, living room furniture, 85-inch television, dining room tables and chairs, and even an air fryer. It was like a mini penthouse. Again, maybe my kids *are* spoiled . . . nah. Spending the day with TJ, making sure my son had everything he needed and knowing he had a lot of influence on how his dorm room looked was definitely a blessing. And while we had great conversations throughout the day and a great embrace, again, it wasn't hard to say goodbye.

I thought it was because he was only a two-hour drive from my house, plus he was living in the same city as WWE's Performance Center/NXT Arena where, on occasion, I go for work. That gave me ample opportunity to meet up with him and grab a meal and a hug.

Then I realized that I would be just as okay if he were leaving for college in California and it wasn't as easy to see him.

Yes, I missed him, of course.

TJ is one of my three closest friends, the other two obviously being my other son, Titus, and my daughter, Leah.

TJ is one of my running mates, and sometimes sitting mate; he's someone who is always up for jumping on a plane to see a concert, even a country one, or sitting on the couch and watching a favorite show or listening to music. I often took my television pop culture cues from TJ. He introduced me to new shows like *Outer Banks*, *Ozark*, and *Who Killed Sara?*

But as much as I missed him, I was more excited for him. I was excited that he would be a student athlete at a Division I college.

I was excited that he had set his mind to accomplish a goal and had succeeded.

I was excited that he was living the life that he chose. Football was the sport that he chose. Linebacker was the position that he chose. The University of Central Florida was the institute of higher learning that he chose. It was his life, not a life that I picked out for him.

I was so excited about him moving further down the path to adulthood and a career and all the spoils that come with those.

And once I realized all of that, I had a clear revelation as to why I was okay with him leaving the nest.

It was because I knew that I did not have to worry about him going out and making silly choices. I knew that I would not receive a call that my son had been driving while drunk or had been disrespectful to the coaches. I knew that he would study hard and take care of his health. I knew and knew and knew so much about my son that I did not have to worry about anything.

No parent can prepare for the day that a child leaves the nest.

We are all going to miss our children, even when we know they are no longer children.

What makes it easier, however, is when we know that they are prepared to be on their own because we prepared them for that transition.

I prepared TJ and am preparing Titus and Leah with the basics. They know how to cook, clean, do laundry, and all the other chores that come with taking care of oneself. Well, actually, TJ is not that great of a cook, and Titus doesn't like it that much. The verdict is still out on Leah. She has never cooked anything for me.

I helped each of my children develop a work ethic, understand what it means to be good winners and losers, learn how to handle racism to the best of their abilities, and know the importance of putting the student in student athlete, and countless other lessons.

I taught them that family matters, and I developed a strong enough bond with each that I know none of them will ever ghost me, even if they move to the farthest corner of the Earth.

I taught them how to handle themselves around people of all colors, creeds, and financial classes.

I taught them how to handle themselves around jerks, haters, bullies, and in just about every situation.

I taught them to be respectful of others, even those they don't like.

When our kids are little babies, it's hard to envision that they will never not need us to do everything for them. But our job as parents is to prepare them to handle anything and everything without us.

That is why I immediately was able to handle myself as a student at the University of Florida, whereas I had previously been unprepared to handle change. My dad, Mr. Blalock, took me under his tutelage and prepared me. My mother was, remains, and will always be a great parent—not a perfect parent, but a great parent. But I needed that strong male role model to thrive. He taught me to be a great man—not a great Black man, not a great athlete or star, but a great man, period.

Yes, I miss TJ. Yes, I will miss Titus and Leah. But I'm not worried about them leaving the nest because I know they are prepared.

That is all that we can do.

CHAPTER 11

LEGACY

While my father, Mr. Blalock, was superintendent of Suwannee County from 1988 to 1996, Suwannee High School athletics enjoyed incredible success: three consecutive football state championships and two wrestling championships plus major renovations to their football stadium and wrestling room.

After leaving that position, as I previously wrote, he went on to serve as superintendent of Hamilton County from 2000 to 2004.

In retirement, he continued to attend education conferences throughout the state. And when he did, there was typically someone hoping to meet with him. Sometimes it was a former student. Sometimes it was the child of a former student who had heard of him. Sometimes it was someone who was linked to my father's athletic achievements (he also coached several championship basketball teams over the years). But, primarily, the person's connection to my father was much deeper than sports.

By bringing me into his home and taking me in as a son, my father may have helped me the most, but he helped countless others as well. He purchased clothes for kids, provided meals for students' families, and helped parents get jobs. He would begin helping some families when the student was a child and continue to support them for as long as it took, often until that student and their family could stand on their own with pride. And he was always willing to risk his own career to do what was right for a child.

Two stories stand out.

As a basketball coach, my father demanded that players wore shirts and ties to school on game day. If they could not afford such clothes, he helped. He wanted players to walk the hallways with pride, distinguish themselves from the rest of the student body, and look like leaders.

Well, he had a principal who, for whatever reason, did not support my father's vision for the players. So to prove a point, one game day, the principal demanded that a player dig some school flower beds while wearing his shirt and tie. The player went right to my father, who told him to sit tight while he took care of the situation.

My father stormed into the principal's office. The two were screaming at one another, face-to-face, like an umpire and Major League Baseball manager. In anger, the principal grabbed a pack of cigarettes from his pocket and threw them at my dad's feet. Well, my father then threw down the gauntlet. "If one of those cigarettes rolls into my foot, I'm going to knock the hell out of you," he declared to the principal. The principal responded by suspending my father for three days, but the player did not have to dig those flower beds. So you tell me who won?

Another time, during the summer, my father spotted a little kid with a freshly swollen eye and bloodied face. When my dad inquired about what happened, the child responded that he was playing in a field owned by a white school board member who did not want him there. So the school board member made that clear by beating him up.

I'm sure by now you know how my heroic father responded. Yep, he stormed over to that field to confront the man. In his angriest scowl, my father said that he was taking the kid to the hospital and that he would be back with the bill for the man to pay. My father did return. And that school board member did pay.

A year later, as schools were being integrated, my father was offered the job of principal, overseeing both white and Black elementary students. It turned out that the deciding vote came from that same school board member whom my father had confronted. He put their differences aside, knowing that my father would look out for all those kids during the difficult transition.

I have long known that my father has had a superhero-sized impact on my life. If there is a Black Superman, in my eyes, it's my father. But the full impact that he has had on me is now becoming clearer than ever.

I have never been a go-with-the-flow type of guy. Even as a kid, I always went against everything and anything that seemed to be logical to a normal human being. I don't apologize for that. It's why I have been able to achieve and accomplish so many things, especially in the world of philanthropy. As an adult, like my father and with lessons he passed on to me, I have harnessed my rebellious attitude for the good of others. As a father and as a community leader, I have never wanted to do anything that is normal, because the norm will only get you so far. To change things, you must be willing to do things that others might think are crazy to dream up and impossible to accomplish. You must be willing to buck the system when you know that doing so is in the best interest of others. That is what my father did and passed on to me.

That attitude is how I have been able to change the school that bears my name. It's the first of its kind in Hillsborough County, but hopefully not the last. Hopefully, others see what I, with the help of so many, have been able to accomplish at my school. I hope that others then realize that they too can do the same with heart, desire, and passion.

For me, everything starts with God providing me a vision for what I should do. It's very difficult for a lot of people to push through, to fight through the difficulties of carrying out a vision. For me, there have always been challenges and naysayers and people who seem intent on stopping me for whatever reason. But like my father, I have endured by looking past the fight and the immediate challenge to see the vision coming to fruition. Only then do you realize that the fight is worth it.

I will not share those specific challenges in this book. I will only say that money has been stolen from good causes and people have tried to sully my name by saying things like that I only do good deeds for the accolades.

There is no need to be more specific and sully other people's names in return, for as Proverbs 4:25-27 says, "Let your eyes look straight ahead; fix your gaze directly before you. Give careful thought to the paths for your feet and be steadfast in all your ways. Don't turn to the right or the left; keep your foot from evil."

But I do share all of my struggles with my children. I want them to understand why I might be in a certain mood. But I more so want them to understand what it takes to make a difference. You have to be willing to brush off the criticism and move past the bad actors. Sometimes, you have to be willing to take that three-day suspension as a teacher. Sometimes, you have to be willing to confront that white school board member about their racism. I want my children to have the mindset that people might doubt them, people might question them, people might talk negatively about them, and people might think they have a greedy agenda, but as long as they do exactly what God has called upon them to do, they will come out on top, even in the face of foolishness, outrageousness, and negativity.

Supporting childhood education is God's vision for me, as it was for my father, which is why God likely put the two of us together.

Quality childhood education is not something that is readily available in many underserved communities. Therefore, when those kids enter high school, they do so three or more grade levels behind fellow students who had access to better childhood education.

Sometimes, it's the fault of the elementary and middle school they attended. Quality teachers are not willing to work in the "ghetto." And some of those who are willing do so with the attitude that such kids are unreachable, not teachable, so why try? Other times, the school just doesn't have the resources that other schools have. Tax dollars provide only so much to public schools. They also rely on donations and other forms of support from parents. But in some areas, the parents have neither the money nor time to give. So the school falls behind.

I have always been involved in this fight. As far back as high school, I volunteered to help the underserved kids. Again, I get that from my father.

My current journey, the one that resulted in the Thaddeus M. Bullard Academy, began in 2016 when Ricky Sailor and I discussed how neither of us had had a birthday party as children because our families could not afford to throw one. We then decided to do all that we could to ensure that children growing up like us could celebrate their birthday with a party, even if just once.

So we partnered with a local chicken restaurant called PDQ to throw Champions of Characters birthday parties. Each month, if a child from Sligh Middle Magnet, which had a less fortunate student body, and Pepin Academy, which serves children with disabilities, had had a birthday and had exhibited positive qualities, they were invited to a party in their gymnasium. PDQ supplied the food. I supplied the cake. We all supplied the fun and positive vibes. That quickly morphed into inviting all students who were People of Character that month. Those monthly celebrations were a highlight of my life. But I wondered if I could do more. God showed me the way.

One morning in 2018, I woke early, as I usually do, to get to the gym for a morning workout. On that particular day, I finished around 4:45 a.m., and as I prepared to drive home, God compelled me to take the 20-minute, out-the-way drive to Sligh. I pulled into the parking lot and sat there for another 20 minutes, listening to gospel music, staring at the school, and wondering why I was sent there. I then returned home to get my children ready for their day.

For the next six weeks, I woke even earlier so that I had more time after my morning workout. I continued to sit in the parking lot, listening to gospel music, and waiting for God to tell me what I needed to do. But I also drove around the community where the school is located.

Sligh sits within a zip code that has the sixth highest percentage of children living in poverty in the state of Florida. That seemed impossible in a city like Tampa, which was undergoing such a positive transformation. Downtown's waterfront area was having billions of dollars poured into it, and that prosperity grew outward to the connecting suburbs. Yet Sligh's neighborhood remained relatively ignored.

I also realized that it was only a matter of time before the growth reached Sligh's zip code, but in what form would it arrive? Would the neighborhoods be cleaned up and improved for the current residents? Or would the area be gentrified and see developers push those families out and into another rundown community elsewhere, as seems to be the norm across the country? Such change improves the bricks and mortar of a community but ignores the people who made up that community.

It was around that time that LeBron James was starting his I Promise School, an underserved Akron, Ohio, community's public school supported by the LeBron James Family Foundation. That school provides not just a better education to the students but also wraparound services to lift up the families, such as food pantries for families and GED and job placement for parents. I met with some of those involved with LeBron's school and wondered why we could not do something similar in Tampa.

That, I realized, is something that I *could* do. I have the celebrity. I've made the connections. I have the trust. I have the heart. I have the work ethic.

And just like that, I saw God's vision for me and brought it to the Hillsborough County superintendent. I told him that we can no longer ignore that Sligh is failing its children and community by operating in a standard way. We needed to make changes by thinking outside of the box, by taking risks, by thinking big. I wanted my Bullard Family Foundation to adopt Sligh, I told the superintendent. When my grandfather and father sought to make change, they did so with risk to their health and lives. All we risked was failure. And if the partnership failed to get the job done, the school would be no worse off and at least we would know that we did all that we could. The superintendent gave me the go-ahead.

We needed to improve both the aesthetics and culture of the school.

If kids attend a school that looks like no one cares about it, then they will not care either, nor will some or much of the staff. It needed a new paint job, murals, and better furniture. It needed a turf football field, new track, and new weight room. I wanted the children to attend the same quality of school as those who live in affluent neighborhoods and realize, perhaps for the first time, that they are just as deserving. No, I wanted them to attend a better school so they could see that they can strive for even more.

I wanted the kids to have a place where they could grow and see possibilities. I left the Florida Sheriffs Boys Ranch with a message that I wanted to bring to Sligh: There is no such thing as a bad kid. There are just kids who need more support.

We needed to make sure to put the kids in the best possible position and around the best possible people so they could have a better outcome in the end. That was my focus from the start.

I provided some of the funds but could not do it on my own. That is where my Bullard Family Foundation stepped in. Sligh's neighborhood wasn't completely ignored. It just mostly received one type of positive attention: transactional change, which is when people offer money or in-kind services to provide immediate help, like holiday gifts or food for the hungry. That is necessary, but so is transformational change. That comes through services that transform someone's life, not just their day or week. The I Promise School transforms families by providing the students and families the tools needed to make something of their lives.

Those who spend money for transactional change have their hearts in the right places but perhaps don't have the know-how to make true transformational change. But if they supported my Bullard Family Foundation, we could make those transformational changes at Sligh and in other areas of the community. My goal was to create a space where both the public and private sector could invest in a vision, whether that be through their time, talent, or resources, and make real transformational change.

That has happened, and one by one, I have checked off my wish list.

As for cultural change, little things helped with that. I walked the hallways and hugged the staff and told them that they are appreciated and are making a difference. Kindness spreads like wildfire. Soon, others were doing the same. Some people at the school once believed that the situation at Sligh was helpless. Simply through kindness, that outlook transformed into one of hope.

We also began major school-wide programs.

The Ron Clark Academy, which is a nonprofit middle school in Atlanta that also seeks to make transformational change, have what they call a "house system." I learned that schools in Hillsborough County have one too. It's akin to the houses that compete against one another in the Hogwarts School of Witchcraft and Wizardry in the *Harry Potter* series. Except, rather than magic competitions, the real-life houses have friendly battles in fun athletic events *and* (this is the important part) through kindness and academic challenges. Houses at Sligh have names like the House of Determination and the House of Excellence. Everyone on campus, from the cafeteria workers and teachers to the students, are part of a house and can earn points through competitions, academic achievement, good behavior, and school participation. The house system is meant to bring pride to the campus by promoting pride in oneself and the school as a whole.

It all worked.

After one year, in 2019, Sligh went from an F school to a C.

In October 2021, the school district recognized my work by changing Sligh's name to the Thaddeus M. Bullard Academy at Sligh Middle Magnet School. Around a year later, Suwannee High School's football field was officially named for my dad.

I did not become involved in the school with the end goal of having my name emblazoned on the building, nor did my father defend the player who was told to dig flower beds so that his name would adorn a football field. We did what we did because that is what God called upon us to do. And while no one should expect gratitude for good deeds, it's nice to receive a pat on the back.

My school. My father's football field. Those are just two of the legacies we leave behind to show others what is possible with a big heart, determination, and work ethic.

Our other legacy is our children.

I'm my father's legacy. He shaped me through his words and actions. My life is a direct reflection of his life.

He is a man who gave selflessly to others.

If such a man did not take me in and show me the way, who knows if I would have become a man who also gave selflessly to others.

———

To my fathers, both of them:

I speak a lot about Mr. Blalock in this book and rightfully so. He was the first man I called Dad, and he provided me with an example of what a real man does for his family and his community, and he did so by being the best version of himself. He wasn't perfect, but for me, he was the perfect man to get me to where I needed to be. This book is about raising a child, and he did that for me.

I would be remiss if I did not again mention my other father, my spiritual father, Pastor Gregory Powe Sr., who came into my life at a time in my adulthood when I needed manhood reinvigorated before me. Someday, when the time and topics are right, I hope to write and speak more about him.

God had a plan.

He put me with the right people at the right time.

He put me with fathers like Mr. Blalock and like Pastor Powe. He gave me father figures who doubled as heroes.

Mr. Blalock and Pastor Powe could have been brothers. Both came from the South where racism filled their childhoods. Yet they found a way to transcend that and other barriers. They then found a way to connect people instead of dividing people.

They were led by their morals and convictions. Right, wrong, or indifferent, they stood on those. They believed in themselves, and they believed in what they were called to do.

I now also live by my morals and my convictions. I stand on them.

I too do everything I can to help people and bring people together. God made me a connector simply by how he connected me with the right people at the right time, and not just Mr. Blalock and Pastor Powe, but countless others: Coach Bump, Mr. Monogue, the woman who gave me that remote-controlled car, Dave Bautista, the McMahon family, and many others. Some say right place, right time. I say right people, right time.

My children are now connectors too. Their sweet spirit, their humble approach, and their dignified stance will allow them to grow into superior advocates for whatever cause they choose. Most importantly, they will be great role models for their peers—not perfect role models, but great ones. And while I will not take all of the credit for how my children turn out, I will take pride in knowing that I had a hand in grooming them into some of the greatest human beings on this Earth.

To Mr. Blalock and Pastor Powe, who served as mentors, spiritual leaders, sounding boards: thank you for stepping up to the plate when you did not have to.

And thank you to all the fathers around the globe. Those whom I know and those whom I don't. Your commitment to being the best you can be would truly help this world be a better place and produce some of the greatest human beings of all races and backgrounds.

Being a champion or at the top of any profession requires hard work, dedication, discipline, persistence, lots of long nights and lots of early mornings, some restless days and some restful days. Fatherhood is no different. Fatherhood is a journey. Never forget that. Never forget that at the end of the day, you have an opportunity to make a difference.

Being a champion dad is hard work.

Being a champion father is a high honor.

Dad, Father, Pop, Poppa, or whatever your children choose to call you—all or any of those titles should bring you a great sense of pride as a man. They are the greatest titles in the world.

Thank you too to my children, for not only helping me grow into the man I am today but also for allowing me the space and the time to grow into the man I am today and who I will continue to be. I sincerely hope and pray that you feel a great sense of pride when people mention my name. I hope that I have set examples that you want to pass on to your own children.

With as much pride as I have for you, I pray that I have never caused you shame, disappointment, or embarrassment. And I pray that you will continue to grow in every aspect of life using the lessons that I have tried to teach you over the years. I hope you also never forget the lessons you have learned from your village—your mother, bonus mom, grandparents, aunts and uncles, cousins, friends, and coaches.

The simple words "I love you, Dad," "I'm proud of you, Dad," and "Way to go, Dad" go a long way. A hug goes a long way too. I know that the time will come when the days between hugs grow further apart as life takes us physically farther apart, but I know we will never be separated spiritually or emotionally. Our love will always be there. Our love will always connect us. Our love for one another, through one another, and with one another will continue to grow into others and hopefully spread around the world.

There is no doubt that raising children has been my greatest challenge. But it also provided me with the greatest title, for which I'm sincerely forever grateful.

———

Love,
Dad